THE
Deeper
MEANING
OF
LIFF

Douglas Adams is the creator of *Dirk Gently*, *Last Chance to See* and all four volumes of *The Hitch-Hiker's Guide to the Galaxy* trilogy. He has a magnificent pulverbatch.

John Lloyd is the producer behind *Not the Nine O'Clock News*, *Spitting Image*, *Blackadder* and a number of affcots.

D0104276

THE
Deeper
MEANING
OF
LIFF

DOUGLAS ADAMS
& JOHN LLOYD

illuminated by
BERT KITCHEN

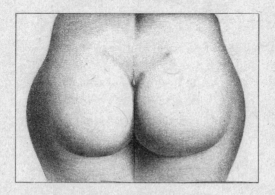

PAN BOOKS
AND
FABER & FABER

First published 1990 by Pan Books Limited and Faber & Faber Limited

This paperback edition published 1992 by
PAN BOOKS LIMITED
a division of Pan Macmillan Publishers Limited
Cavaye Place London SW10 9PG
and Basingstoke
in association with Faber & Faber Limited

Associated companies throughout the world

ISBN 0-330-32220-6

1 3 5 7 9 8 6 4 2

A CIP catalogue record for this book is available from
the British Library

Photoset by Parker Typesetting Service, Leicester
Printed in England by Clays Ltd, St Ives plc

With grateful thanks to Eugen Beer,
Jane Belson, Jon Canter, Alex Catto,
Helen Fielding, Stephen Fry, Gaye Green,
Sean Hardie, PBJ, Helen Rhys Jones,
Laurie Rowley, Peter Spence and Caroline
Warner for some of the more interesting
and repellent ideas in this book.

Contents

—

Prefaces

PREFACE TO THE FIRST EDITION, 1983

In Life* there are many hundreds of common experiences, feelings, situations and even objects which we all know and recognize, but for which no word exists. On the other hand, the world is littered with thousands of spare words which spend their time doing nothing but loafing about on signposts pointing at places. Our job, as we see it, is to get these words down off the signposts and into the mouths of babes and sucklings and so on, where they can start earning their keep in everyday conversation and make a more positive contribution to society. *Douglas Adams, John Lloyd, Malibu, 1982*

PREFACE TO THE 1984 REPRINT

What we said in the first preface pretty much stands, I think.
Douglas Adams, New York, 1983

PREFACE TO THE SECOND 1984 REPRINT

Can't think of any thing much to add to the previous preface. It's nice, here, though. *Douglas Adams, Seychelles, 1984*

Is it? *John Lloyd, Birmingham, 1984*

PREFACE TO THE 1986 REPRINT

There was a point I was going to make in this preface but it's one of those things that you just can't remember when you actually sit down to write it. *Douglas Adams, Madagascar, 1985*

*And, indeed in Liff

PREFACES

PREFACE TO THE 1987 REPRINT

No. It came back to me briefly when I was in Brazil, but I didn't have a pen with me. *Douglas Adams, Hong Kong, 1986*

PREFACE TO THE 1988 REPRINT

Did you get the preface I faxed you from New Zealand?

Douglas Adams, Zaïre, 1988

PREFACE TO THE 1989 REPRINT

No. *John Lloyd, Lambeth, 1989*

PREFACE TO THE SECOND 1989 REPRINT

Pity. That was a good one. Can't remember how it went now.

Douglas Adams, Beijing, 1989

PREFACE TO THE THIRD 1989 REPRINT

Did we make the point about all these words actually being real place names? *Douglas Adams, Mauritius, 1989*

PREFACE TO THE FOURTH 1989 REPRINT

Yes. *John Lloyd, Lambeth, 1989*

PREFACE TO THE FIRST EDITION OF THE DEEPER MEANING OF LIFF 1990

Well, there's not much we need to add to that then, really, is there? *Douglas Adams, John Lloyd, Sydney, 1990*

Maps

A

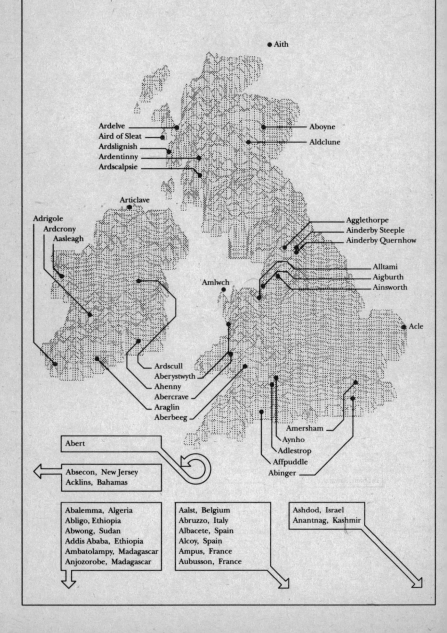

Aith

Ardelve
Aird of Sleat
Ardslignish
Ardentinny
Ardscalpsie

Aboyne
Aldclune

Articlave

Adrigole
Ardcrony
Aasleagh

Agglethorpe
Ainderby Steeple
Ainderby Quernhow

Alltami
Aigburth
Ainsworth

Amlwch

Acle

Ardscull
Aberystwyth
Ahenny
Abercrave
Araglin
Aberbeeg

Amersham
Aynho
Adlestrop
Affpuddle
Abinger

Abert

Absecon, New Jersey
Acklins, Bahamas

Abalemma, Algeria
Abligo, Ethiopia
Abwong, Sudan
Addis Ababa, Ethiopia
Ambatolampy, Madagascar
Anjozorobe, Madagascar

Aalst, Belgium
Abruzzo, Italy
Albacete, Spain
Alcoy, Spain
Ampus, France
Aubusson, France

Ashdod, Israel
Anantnag, Kashmir

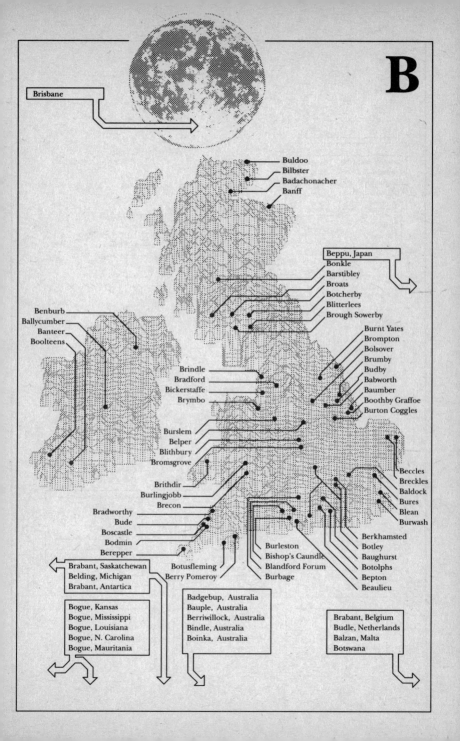

B

Brisbane

Buldoo
Bilbster
Badachonacher
Banff

Beppu, Japan
Bonkle
Barstibley
Broats
Botcherby
Blitterlees
Brough Sowerby

Benburb
Ballycumber
Banteer
Boolteens

Burnt Yates
Brompton
Bolsover
Brumby
Budby
Babworth
Baumber
Boothby Graffoe
Burton Coggles

Brindle
Bradford
Bickerstaffe
Brymbo

Burslem
Belper
Blithbury
Bromsgrove

Beccles
Breckles
Baldock
Bures
Blean
Burwash

Brithdir
Burlingjobb
Brecon

Bradworthy
Bude
Boscastle
Bodmin
Berepper

Burleston
Bishop's Caundle
Blandford Forum
Burbage

Berkhamsted
Botley
Baughurst
Botolphs
Bepton
Beaulieu

Brabant, Saskatchewan
Belding, Michigan
Brabant, Antartica

Botusfleming
Berry Pomeroy

Bogue, Kansas
Bogue, Mississippi
Bogue, Louisiana
Bogue, N. Carolina
Bogue, Mauritania

Badgebup, Australia
Bauple, Australia
Berriwillock, Australia
Bindle, Australia
Boinka, Australia

Brabant, Belgium
Budle, Netherlands
Balzan, Malta
Botswana

C

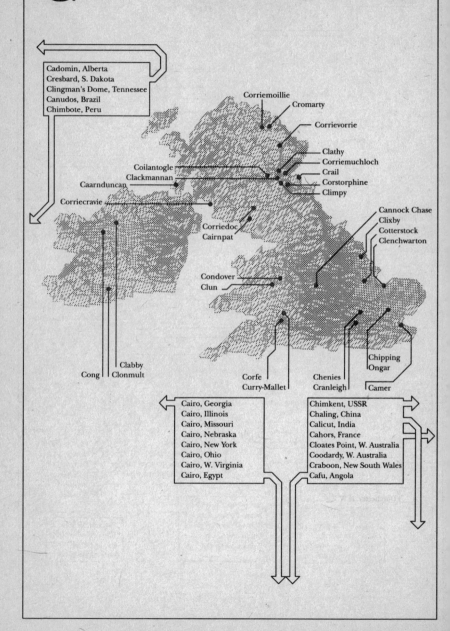

Cadomin, Alberta
Cresbard, S. Dakota
Clingman's Dome, Tennessee
Canudos, Brazil
Chimbote, Peru

Corriemoillie
Cromarty
Corrievorrie
Clathy
Corriemuchloch
Crail
Corstorphine
Climpy
Coilantogle
Clackmannan
Caarnduncan
Corriecravie
Cannock Chase
Clixby
Cotterstock
Clenchwarton
Corriedoc
Cairnpat
Condover
Clun
Chipping
Ongar
Cong Clabby
Clonmult
Corfe
Curry-Mallet
Chenies
Cranleigh
Camer

Cairo, Georgia
Cairo, Illinois
Cairo, Missouri
Cairo, Nebraska
Cairo, New York
Cairo, Ohio
Cairo, W. Virginia
Cairo, Egypt

Chimkent, USSR
Chaling, China
Calicut, India
Cahors, France
Cloates Point, W. Australia
Coodardy, W. Australia
Craboon, New South Wales
Cafu, Angola

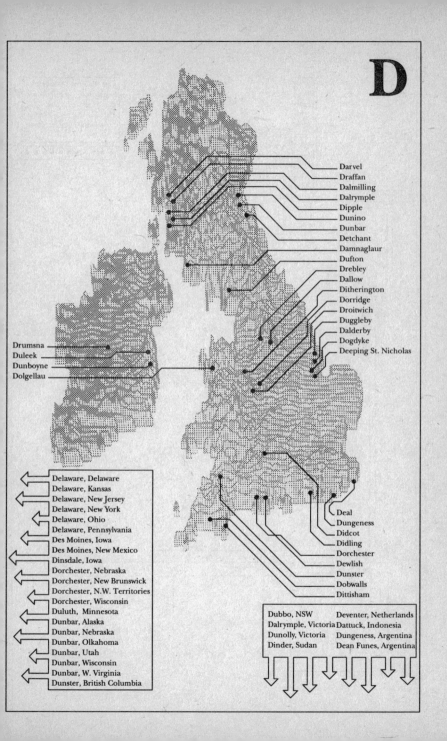

D

Darvel
Draffan
Dalmilling
Dalrymple
Dipple
Dunino
Dunbar
Detchant
Damnaglaur
Dufton
Drebley
Dallow
Ditherington
Dorridge
Droitwich
Duggleby
Dalderby
Dogdyke
Deeping St. Nicholas

Drumsna
Duleek
Dunboyne
Dolgellau

Deal
Dungeness
Didcot
Didling
Dorchester
Dewlish
Dunster
Dobwalls
Dittisham

Delaware, Delaware
Delaware, Kansas
Delaware, New Jersey
Delaware, New York
Delaware, Ohio
Delaware, Pennsylvania
Des Moines, Iowa
Des Moines, New Mexico
Dinsdale, Iowa
Dorchester, Nebraska
Dorchester, New Brunswick
Dorchester, N.W. Territories
Dorchester, Wisconsin
Duluth, Minnesota
Dunbar, Alaska
Dunbar, Nebraska
Dunbar, Olkahoma
Dunbar, Utah
Dunbar, Wisconsin
Dunbar, W. Virginia
Dunster, British Columbia

Dubbo, NSW	Deventer, Netherlands
Dalrymple, Victoria	Dattuck, Indonesia
Dunolly, Victoria	Dungeness, Argentina
Dinder, Sudan	Dean Funes, Argentina

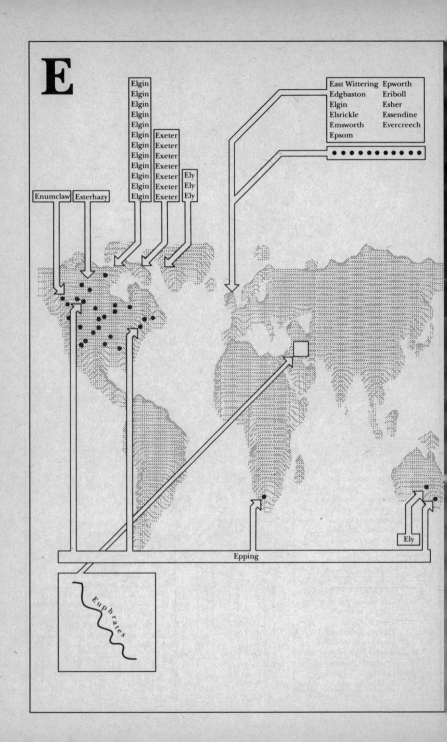

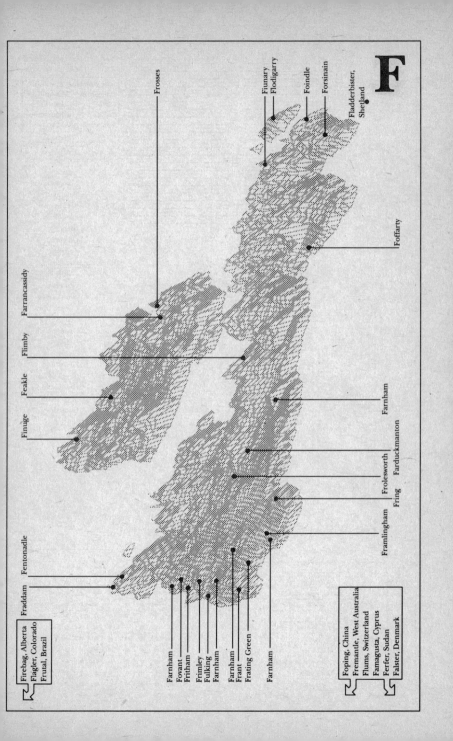

F

Frosses

Fiunary
Flodigarry
Foindle
Forsinain
Fladderbister, Shetland

Foffarry

Farrancassidy

Flimby

Feakle

Finuge

Farnham

Farduckmanton

Frolesworth

Fring

Framlingham

Fentonadle

Fraddam

Farnham
Fovant
Fritham
Frimley
Fulking
Farnham

Farnham
Frant
Frating Green

Farnham

Firebag, Alberta
Flagler, Colorado
Fruial, Brazil

Foping, China
Fremantle, West Australia
Flums, Switzerland
Famagusta, Cyprus
Ferfer, Sudan
Falster, Denmark

G

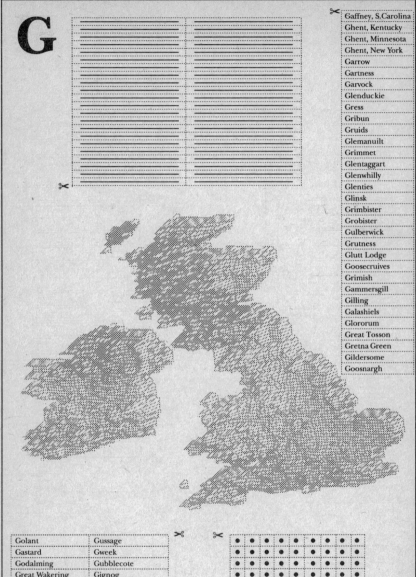

H

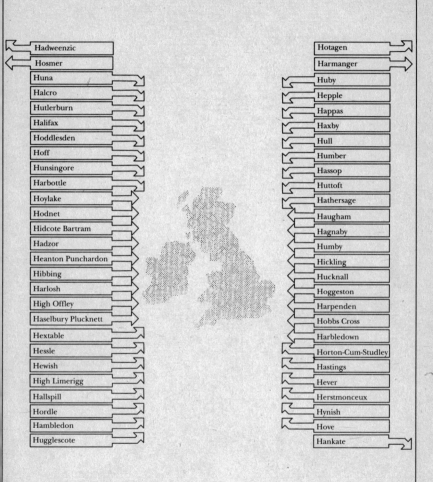

Hadweenzic

Hosmer

Huna

Halcro

Hutlerburn

Halifax

Hoddlesden

Hoff

Hunsingore

Harbottle

Hoylake

Hodnet

Hidcote Bartram

Hadzor

Heanton Punchardon

Hibbing

Harlosh

High Offley

Haselbury Plucknett

Hextable

Hessle

Hewish

High Limerigg

Hallspill

Hordle

Hambledon

Hugglescote

Hotagen

Harmanger

Huby

Hepple

Happas

Haxby

Hull

Humber

Hassop

Huttoft

Hathersage

Haugham

Hagnaby

Humby

Hickling

Hucknall

Hoggeston

Harpenden

Hobbs Cross

Harbledown

Horton-Cum-Studley

Hastings

Hever

Herstmonceux

Hynish

Hove

Hankate

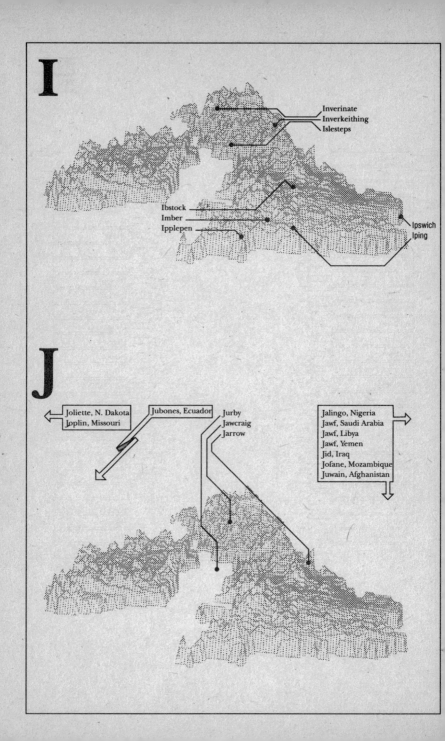

I

Inverinate
Inverkeithing
Islesteps

Ibstock
Imber
Ipplepen

Ipswich
Iping

J

Joliette, N. Dakota
Joplin, Missouri

Jubones, Ecuador

Jurby
Jawcraig
Jarrow

Jalingo, Nigeria
Jawf, Saudi Arabia
Jawf, Libya
Jawf, Yemen
Jid, Iraq
Jofane, Mozambique
Juwain, Afghanistan

K

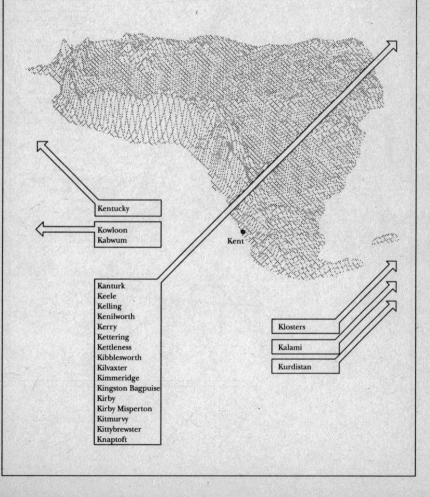

Kentucky

Kowloon
Kabwum

Kent

Kanturk
Keele
Kelling
Kenilworth
Kerry
Kettering
Kettleness
Kibblesworth
Kilvaxter
Kimmeridge
Kingston Bagpuise
Kirby
Kirby Misperton
Kitmurvy
Kittybrewster
Knaptoft

Klosters

Kalami

Kurdistan

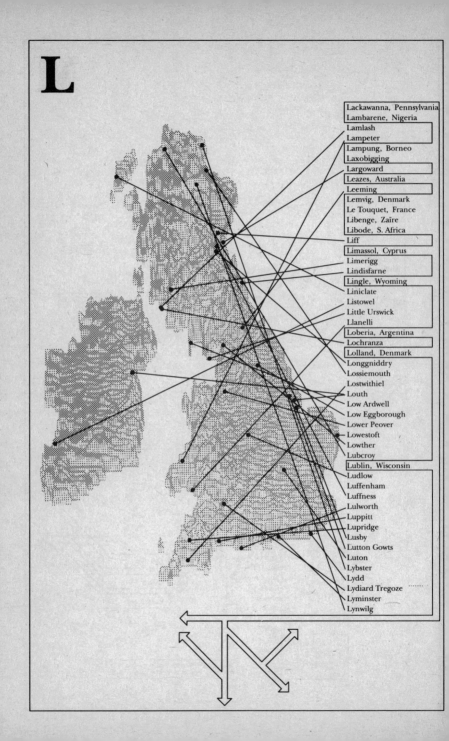

L

Lackawanna, Pennsylvania
Lambarene, Nigeria
Lamlash
Lampeter
Lampung, Borneo
Laxobigging
Largoward
Leazes, Australia
Leeming
Lemvig, Denmark
Le Touquet, France
Libenge, Zaïre
Libode, S. Africa
Liff
Limassol, Cyprus
Limerigg
Lindisfarne
Lingle, Wyoming
Liniclate
Listowel
Little Urswick
Llanelli
Loberia, Argentina
Lochranza
Lolland, Denmark
Longgniddry
Lossiemouth
Lostwithiel
Louth
Low Ardwell
Low Eggborough
Lower Peover
Lowestoft
Lowther
Lubcroy
Lublin, Wisconsin
Ludlow
Luffenham
Luffness
Lulworth
Luppitt
Lupridge
Lusby
Lutton Gowts
Luton
Lybster
Lydd
Lydiard Tregoze
Lyminster
Lynwilg

M

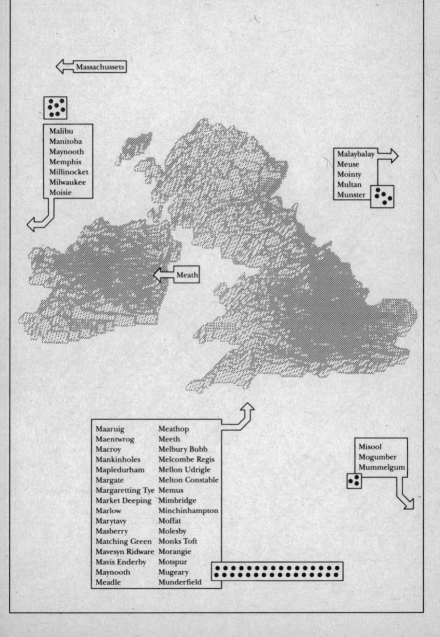

← Massachussets

Malibu
Manitoba
Maynooth
Memphis
Millinocket
Milwaukee
Moisie

Malaybalay →
Meuse
Mointy
Multan
Munster

← Meath

Maaruig   Meathop
Maentwrog   Meeth
Macroy   Melbury Bubb
Mankinholes   Melcombe Regis
Mapledurham   Mellon Udrigle
Margate   Melton Constable
Margaretting Tye Memus
Market Deeping   Mimbridge
Marlow   Minchinhampton
Marytavy   Moffat
Masberry   Molesby
Matching Green   Monks Toft
Mavesyn Ridware Morangie
Mavis Enderby   Motspur
Maynooth   Mugeary
Meadle   Munderfield

Misool
Mogumber
Mummelgum

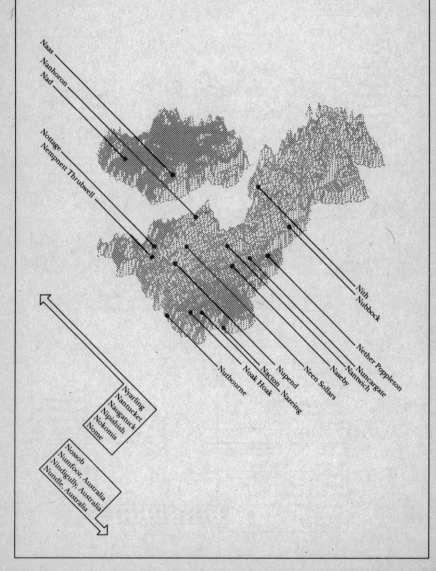

N

Naas
Nanhoron
Nad

Nottage
Nempnett Thrubwell

Nith
Nubbock

Nether Poppleton

Nuncargate
Nantwich
Naseby
Neen Sollars

Nupend

Nacton
Nazeing

Noak Hoak

Nutbourne

Nyarling
Nantucket
Naugatuck
Nipishish
Nokomis
Nome

Nossob
Numfoor, Australia
Nindigully, Australia
Nundle, Australia

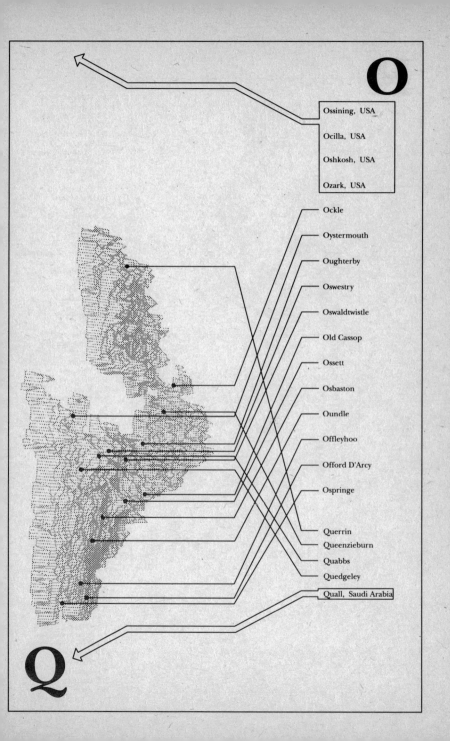

O

Ossining, USA

Ocilla, USA

Oshkosh, USA

Ozark, USA

Ockle

Oystermouth

Oughterby

Oswestry

Oswaldtwistle

Old Cassop

Ossett

Osbaston

Oundle

Offleyhoo

Offord D'Arcy

Ospringe

Querrin

Queenzieburn

Quabbs

Quedgeley

Quall, Saudi Arabia

Q

P

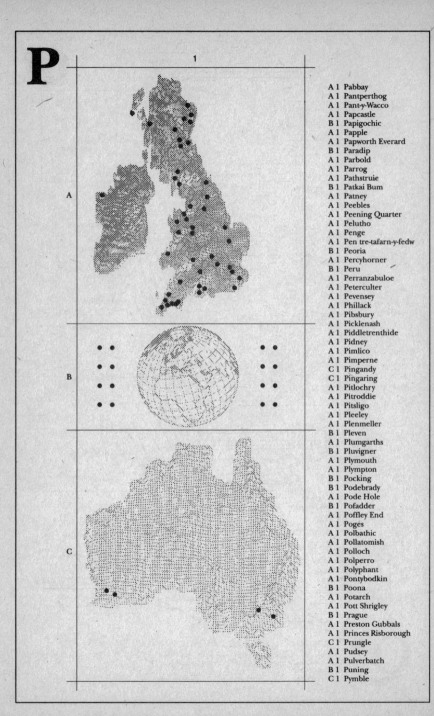

1

A 1 Pabbay
A 1 Pantperthog
A 1 Pant-y-Wacco
A 1 Papcastle
B 1 Papigochic
A 1 Papple
A 1 Papworth Everard
B 1 Paradip
A 1 Parbold
A 1 Parrog
A 1 Pathstruie
B 1 Patkai Bum
A 1 Patney
A 1 Peebles
A 1 Peening Quarter
A 1 Pelutho
A 1 Penge
A 1 Pen tre-tafarn-y-fedw
B 1 Peoria
A 1 Percyhorner
B 1 Peru
A 1 Perranzabuloe
A 1 Peterculter
A 1 Pevensey
A 1 Phillack
A 1 Pibsbury
A 1 Picklenash
A 1 Piddletrenthide
A 1 Pidney
A 1 Pimlico
A 1 Pimperne
C 1 Pingandy
C 1 Pingaring
A 1 Pitlochry
A 1 Pitroddie
A 1 Pitsligo
A 1 Pleeley
A 1 Plenmeller
B 1 Pleven
A 1 Plumgarths
B 1 Pluvigner
A 1 Plymouth
A 1 Plympton
B 1 Pocking
B 1 Podebrady
A 1 Pode Hole
B 1 Pofadder
A 1 Poffley End
A 1 Poges
A 1 Polbathic
A 1 Pollatomish
A 1 Polloch
A 1 Polperro
A 1 Polyphant
A 1 Pontybodkin
B 1 Poona
A 1 Potarch
A 1 Pott Shrigley
B 1 Prague
A 1 Preston Gubbals
A 1 Princes Risborough
C 1 Prungle
A 1 Pudsey
A 1 Pulverbatch
B 1 Puning
C 1 Pymble

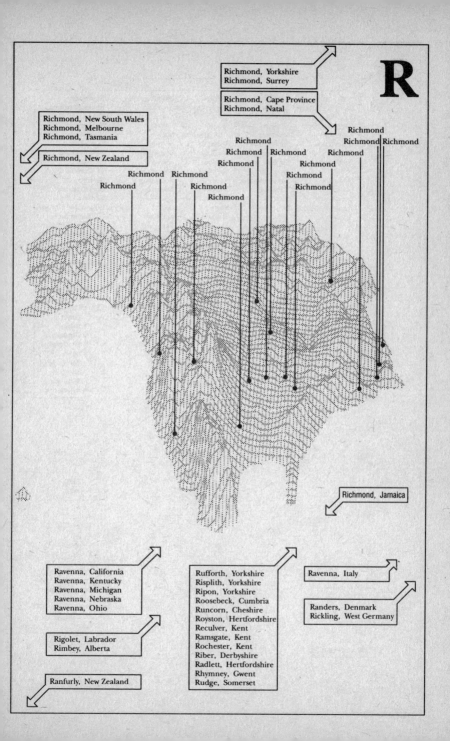

R

Richmond, Yorkshire
Richmond, Surrey

Richmond, Cape Province
Richmond, Natal

Richmond, New South Wales
Richmond, Melbourne
Richmond, Tasmania

Richmond, New Zealand

Richmond
Richmond Richmond
Richmond   Richmond   Richmond   Richmond
Richmond   Richmond
Richmond   Richmond   Richmond
Richmond
Richmond   Richmond
Richmond   Richmond
Richmond

Richmond, Jamaica

Ravenna, California
Ravenna, Kentucky
Ravenna, Michigan
Ravenna, Nebraska
Ravenna, Ohio

Rufforth, Yorkshire
Risplith, Yorkshire
Ripon, Yorkshire
Roosebeck, Cumbria
Runcorn, Cheshire
Royston, Hertfordshire
Reculver, Kent
Ramsgate, Kent
Rochester, Kent
Riber, Derbyshire
Radlett, Hertfordshire
Rhymney, Gwent
Rudge, Somerset

Ravenna, Italy

Randers, Denmark
Rickling, West Germany

Rigolet, Labrador
Rimbey, Alberta

Ranfurly, New Zealand

S

Sadberge	Screggan	Sidcup	Slumbay	Stebbing
Saffron Walden	Scremby	Sigglesthorne	Smarden	Stelling Minnis
Samalaman	Scridain	Silloth	Smearisary	Stibb
Satterthwaite	Scroggs	Simprim	Smisby	Stibbard
Savernake	Scronkey	Sittingbourne	Sneem	Stody
Scackleton	Scullet	Skegness	Snitter	Stoke Poges
Scamblesby	Scurlage	Skellister	Snitterfield	Stowting
Scethrog	Shalunt	Skellow	Snitterby	Strubby
Sconser	Shanklin	Skenfrith	Solent	Stutton
Scopwick	Sheepy Magna	Sketty	Sompting	Sturry
Scorrier	Sheppey	Skibbereen	Sotterley	Suckley Knowl
Scosthrop	Shifnal	Skulamus	Spiddle	Surby
Scrabby	Shimpling	Sligo	Spittal of Glenshee	Sutton and Cheam
Scrabster	Shirmers	Slogarie	Spofforth	Swaffham Bulbeck
Scramoge	Shoeburyness	Sloothby	Spreakley	Swanage
Scraptoft	Shottle	Slubbery	Sproston Green	Swanibost
Screeb	Shrivenham	Sluggan	Staplow	Swefling
				Symond's Yat

Shrenk
Sicamous
Skannerup
Skrubburdnut
Silesia
Slettnut
Slipchitsy
Slobozia
Sloinge
Soller
Steenhuffel
Strassgang

Seattle
Scranton
Scugog
Shenandoah
Skagway
Smyrna
Snover
Southwick
Spoffard
Spokane
Spruce Knob
Spurger
Spuzzum
Squibnocket

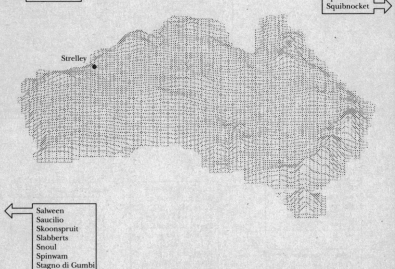

Strelley

Salween
Saucilio
Skoonspruit
Slabberts
Snoul
Spinwam
Stagno di Gumbi

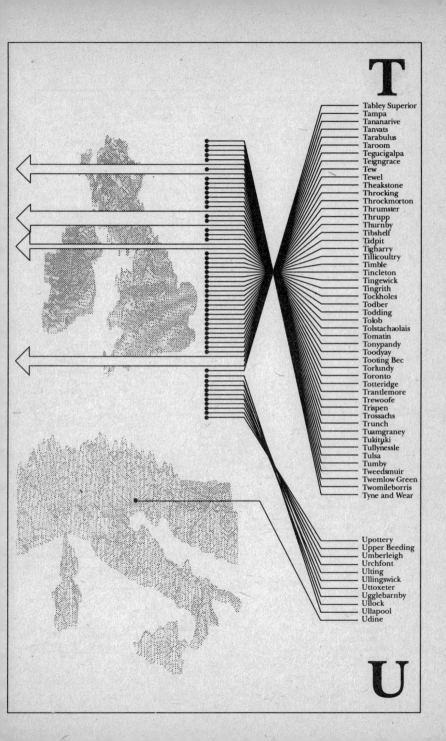

T

Tabley Superior
Tampa
Tananarive
Tanvats
Tarabulus
Taroom
Tegucigalpa
Teigngrace
Tew
Tewel
Theakstone
Throcking
Throckmorton
Thrumster
Thrupp
Thurnby
Tibshelf
Tidpit
Tigharry
Tillicoultry
Timble
Tincleton
Tingewick
Tingrith
Tockholes
Todber
Todding
Tolob
Tolstachaolais
Tomatin
Tonypandy
Toodyay
Tooting Bec
Torlundy
Toronto
Totteridge
Trantlemore
Trewoofe
Trispen
Trossachs
Trunch
Tuamgraney
Tukituki
Tullynessle
Tulsa
Tumby
Tweedsmuir
Twemlow Green
Twomileborris
Tyne and Wear

Upottery
Upper Beeding
Umberleigh
Urchfont
Ulting
Ullingswick
Uttoxeter
Ugglebarnby
Ullock
Ullapool
Udine

U

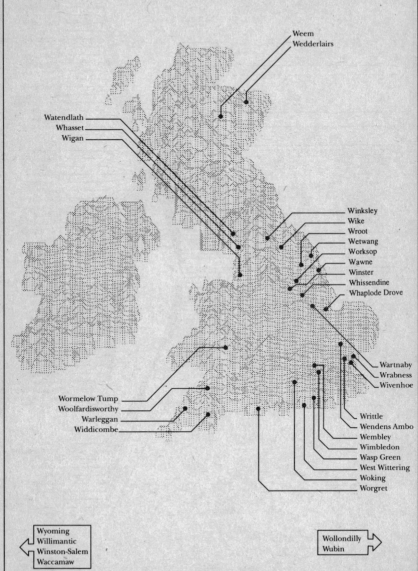

W

Weem
Wedderlairs

Watendlath
Whasset
Wigan

Winksley
Wike
Wroot
Wetwang
Worksop
Wawne
Winster
Whissendine
Whaplode Drove

Wartnaby
Wrabness
Wivenhoe

Wormelow Tump
Woolfardisworthy
Warleggan
Widdicombe

Writtle
Wendens Ambo
Wembley
Wimbledon
Wasp Green
West Wittering
Woking
Worgret

Wyoming
Willimantic
Winston-Salem
Waccamaw

Wollondilly
Wubin

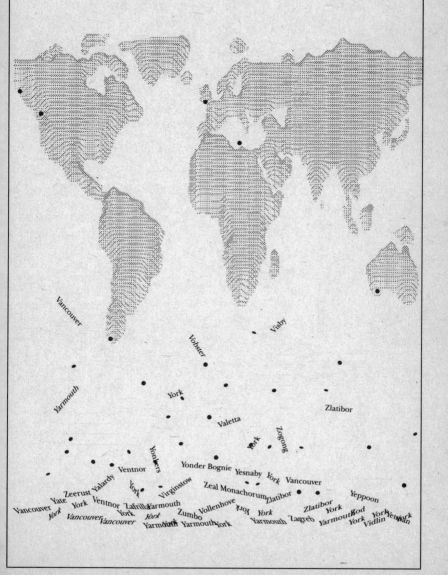

V Y Z

The Deeper Meaning of Liff

A

Aalst (n.)

One who changes his name to be nearer the front.

Aasleagh (n.)

A liqueur made only for drinking at the end of a revoltingly long bottle party when all the drinkable drink has been drunk.

Abalemma (n.)

The agonizing situation in which there is only one possible decision but you still can't take it.

Aberbeeg (vb.)

Of amateur actors, to adopt a Mexican accent when called upon to play any variety of foreigner (except Pakistanis – for whom a Welsh accent is considered sufficient).

Abercrave (vb.)

To desire strongly to swing from the pole on the rear footplate of a bus.

Abert (vb.)

To change a baby's name at the last possible moment.

Aberystwyth (n.)

A nostalgic yearning which is in itself more pleasant than the thing being yearned for.

Abilene (adj.)

Descriptive of the pleasing coolness on the reverse side of the pillow.

Abinger (n.)

One who washes up everything except the frying pan, the cheese-grater and the saucepan which the chocolate sauce has been made in.

Abligo (n.)

One who prides himself on not even knowing what day of the week it is.

Aboyne (vb.)

To beat an expert at a game of skill by playing so appallingly that none of his clever tactics or strategies are of any use to him.

Abruzzo (n.)

The worn patch of ground under a swing.

Absecon (n.)

An annual conference held at the Dragonara Hotel, Leeds, for people who haven't got any other conferences to go to.

Abwong (vb.)

To bounce cheerfully on a bed.

Acklins (pl.n.)

The odd twinges you get in parts of your body when you scratch other parts.

Acle (n.)

The rogue pin which shirtmakers conceal in a hidden fold of a new shirt. Its function is to stab you when you don the garment.

Addis Ababa (n.)

The torrent of incomprehensible gibberish which emanates from the loudspeakers on top of cars covered in stickers.

Adlestrop (n.)

The part of a suitcase which is designed to get snarled up

on conveyor belts at airports. Some of the more modern adlestrop designs have a special 'quick release' feature which enables the case to flip open at this point and fling your underclothes into the conveyor belt's gearing mechanism.

Adrigole (n.)

The centre piece of a merry-go-round on which the man with the tickets stands unnervingly still.

Affcot (n.)

The sort of fart you hope people will talk after.

Affpuddle (n.)

A puddle which is hidden under a pivoted paving stone. You only know it's there when you step on the paving stone and the puddle shoots up your leg.

Ahenny (adj.)

The way people stand when examining other people's bookshelves.

Aigburth (n.)

Any piece of readily identifiable anatomy found amongst cooked meat.

Ainderby Quernhow (n.)

One who continually bemoans the 'loss' of the word 'gay' to the English language, even though they had never used the word in any context at all until they started complaining that they couldn't use it any more.

Ainderby Steeple (n.)

One who asks you a question with the apparent motive of wanting to hear your answer, but who cuts short your opening sentence by leaning forward and saying 'and I'll tell you why I ask . . .' and then talking solidly for the next hour.

Ainsworth (n.)

The length of time it takes to get served in a camera shop.

Hence, also, how long we will have to wait for the abolition of income tax or the Second Coming.

Aird of Sleat (n.)

(Archaic) Ancient Scottish curse placed from afar on the stretch of land now occupied by Heathrow Airport.

Aith (n.)

The single bristle that sticks out sideways on a cheap paintbrush.

Albacete (n.)

A single surprisingly long hair growing in the middle of nowhere.

Albuquerque (n.)

The shapeless squiggle which is utterly unlike your normal signature, but which is, nevertheless, all you are able to produce when asked formally to identify yourself. Muslims, whose religion forbids the making of graven images, use albuquerques to decorate their towels, menu cards and pyjamas.

Alcoy (adj.)

Wanting to be bullied into having another drink.

Aldclune (n.)

One who collects ten-year-old telephone directories.

Alltami (n.)

The ancient art of being able to balance the hot and cold shower taps.

Ambatolampy (n.)

The bizarre assortment of objects collected by a sleepwalker.

Ambleside (n.)

The talk given about the Facts of Life by a father to his son whilst walking in the garden on a Sunday afternoon.

Amersham (n.)

The sneeze which tickles but never comes. (Thought to derive from the Metropolitan Line tube station of the same name where the rails always rattle but the train never arrives.)

Amlwch (n.)

A British Rail sandwich which has been kept soft by being regularly washed and resealed in clingfilm.

Ampus (n.)

A lurid bruise which you can't remember getting.

Anantnag (vb.)

(Eskimo term) To bang your thumbs between the oars when rowing.

Anjozorobe (n.)

A loose, coloured garment someone brings you back from their travels which they honestly expect you to wear.

Araglin (n.)

(Archaic) The medieval practical joke played by young squires on a knight aspirant the afternoon he is due to start his vigil. As the knight arrives at the castle the squires suddenly attempt to raise the drawbridge as the knight and his charger step on it.

Ardcrony (n.)

A remote acquaintance passed off as 'a very good friend of mine' by someone trying to impress people.

Ardelve (vb.)

To make a big display of searching all your pockets when approached by a charity collector.

Ardentinny (n.)

One who rubs his hands eagerly together when he sits down in a restaurant.

Ardslignish (adj.)

Descriptive of the behaviour of Sellotape when you are tired.

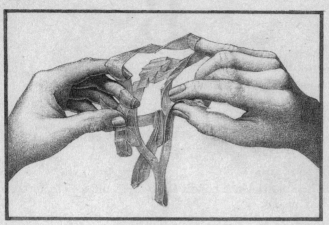

ARDSLIGNISH

Articlave (n.)

A clever architectural construction designed to give the illusion from the top deck of a bus that it is far too big for the road.

Ashdod (n.)

Any object against which a smoker habitually knocks out his pipe.

Aubusson (n.)

The hairstyle a girl adopts for a special occasion which suddenly gives you a sense of what she will look like in twenty years' time.

Aynho (vb.)

Of waiters, never to have a pen.

B

Babworth (n.)

Something which justifies having a really good cry.

Badachonacher (n.)

An on-off relationship which never gets resolved.

Badgebup (n.)

The splotch on a child's face where the ice-cream cone has missed.

Baldock (n.)

The sharp prong on top of a tree stump where the tree has snapped off before being completely sawn through.

Balemartine (n.)

The look which says, 'Stop talking to that woman at once.'

Ballycumber (n.)

One of the six half-read books lying somewhere in your bed.

Balzan (n.)

The noise of a dustbin lid coming off in the middle of the night.

Banff (adj.)

Pertaining to, or descriptive of, that kind of facial expression which is impossible to achieve except when having a passport photograph taken, which results in happas (q.v.).

Banteer (n.)

(Archaic) A lusty and raucous old ballad sung after a particularly spectacular araglin (q.v.) has been pulled off.

Barstibley (n.)

A humorous device such as a china horse or small naked porcelain infant which jocular hosts use to piss water into your Scotch with.

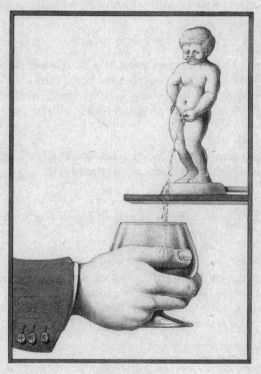

BARSTIBLEY

Bathel (vb.)

To pretend to have read the book under discussion when in fact you've only seen the TV series.

Baughurst (n.)

That kind of large fierce ugly woman who owns a small fierce ugly dog.

Baumber (n.)

A fitted elasticated bottom sheet which turns your mattress banana-shaped.

Bauple (n.)

An indeterminate pustule which could be either a spot or a bite.

Bealings (pl.n.)

(Archaic) The unsavoury parts of a moat which a knight has to pour out of his armour after being the victim of an araglin (q.v.). In medieval Flanders, soup made from bealings was a very slightly sought-after delicacy.

Beaulieu Hill (n.)

The optimum vantage point from which to view people undressing in the bedroom across the street.

Beccles (pl.n.)

The small bone buttons placed in bacon sandwiches by unemployed dentists.

Bedfont (n.)

A lurching sensation in the pit of the stomach experienced at breakfast in a hotel, occasioned by the realization that it is about now that the chambermaid will have discovered the embarrassing stain on your bottom sheet.

Belding (n.)

The technical name for a stallion after its first ball has been cut off. Any notice which reads 'Beware of the Belding' should be taken very, very seriously.

Belper (n.)

A knob of someone else's chewing gum which you unexpectedly find your hand resting on under the passenger seat of your car or on somebody's thigh under their skirt.

Benburb (n.)

The sort of man who becomes a returning officer.

Beppu (n.)

The triumphant slamming shut of a book after reading the final page.

Bepton (n.)

One who beams benignly after burping.

Berepper (n.)

The irrevocable and sturdy fart released in the presence of royalty, which sounds like quite a small motorbike passing by (but not enough to be confused with one).

Berkhamsted (n.)

The massive three-course midmorning blow-out enjoyed by a dieter who has already done his or her slimming duty by having a spoonful of cottage cheese for breakfast.

Berriwillock (n.)

An unknown workmate who writes 'All the best' on your leaving card.

Berry Pomeroy (n.)

1. The shape of a gourmet's lips.
2. The droplet of saliva which hangs from them.

Bickerstaffe (n.)

The person in an office that everyone whinges about in the pub. Many large corporations deliberately employ bickerstaffes in each department. For example, Mr Robert Maxwell was both Chairman and Chief Bickerstaffe of Mirror Group Newspapers.

Bilbster (n.)

A bauple (q.v.) so hideous and enormous that you have to

cover it with sticking plaster and pretend you've cut yourself shaving.

Bindle (vb.)

To slip foreign coins into a customer's change.

Bishop's Caundle (n.)

An opening gambit before a game of chess whereby the missing pieces are replaced by small ornaments from the mantelpiece.

Blandford Forum (n.)

Any Radio 4 chat show.

Blean (n.)

Scientific measure of luminosity: 1 glimmer = 100,000 bleans.

Usherettes' torches are designed to produce between 2.5 and 4 bleans, enabling them to assist you in falling downstairs, treading on people or putting your hand into a Neapolitan tub when reaching for change.

Blithbury (n.)

A look someone gives you which indicates that they're much too drunk to have understood anything you've said to them in the last twenty minutes.

Blitterlees (pl.n.)

The little slivers of bamboo picked off a cane chair by a nervous guest which litter the carpet beneath and tell the chair's owner that the whole piece of furniture is about to uncoil terribly and slowly until it resembles a giant pencil sharpening.

Bodmin (n.)

The irrational and inevitable discrepancy between the amount pooled and the amount needed when a large group of people try to pay a bill together after a meal.

Bogue (n.)

The expanse of skin that appears between the top of your

socks and the bottom of your trousers when you sit down.

'The Duke of Ilford threw himself onto the chesterfield, brazenly displaying his bogues to the dowager Lady Ingatestone.' (*Come Soon, Strange Horseman*, by Barbara Cartland)

Boinka (n.)

The noise through the wall which tells you that the people next door enjoy a better sex life than you do.

Bolsover (n.)

One of those brown plastic trays with bumps on, placed upside down in boxes of chocolates to make you think you're getting two layers.

Bonkle (vb.)

Of plumbing in old hotels, to make loud and unexplained noises in the night, particularly at about five o'clock in the morning.

Boolteens (pl.n.)

The small scatterings of foreign coins and halfpennies which inhabit dressing tables. Since they are never used and never thrown away boolteens account for a significant drain on the world's money supply.

Boothby Graffoe (n.)

The man in the pub who slaps people on the back as if they were old friends, when in fact he has no friends, largely on account of this habit.

Boscastle (n.)

The huge pyramid of tin cans placed just inside the entrance to a supermarket.

Boseman (n.)

One who spends all day loafing about near pedestrian crossings looking as if he's about to cross.

Botcherby (n.)

The principle by which British roads are signposted.

Botley (n.)

The prominent stain on a man's trouser crotch seen on his return from the lavatory. A botley proper is caused by an accident with the push taps, and should not be confused with any stain caused by insufficient waggling of the willy (see piddletrenthide).

Botolphs (pl.n.)

Huge benign tumours which archdeacons and old chemistry teachers affect to wear on the sides of their noses.

Botswana (n.)

Something which is more fruitfully used for a purpose other than that for which it was designed. A fishknife used to lever open a stubborn tin of emulsion is a fine example of a botswana.

Botusfleming (n.)

(Medical) A small, long-handled steel trowel used by surgeons to remove the contents of a patient's nostrils prior to a sinus operation.

Brabant (adj.)

Very much inclined to see how far you can push someone.

Bradford (n.)

A schoolteacher's old hairy jacket, now severely discoloured by chalk dust, ink, egg and the precipitations of unedifying chemical reactions.

Bradworthy (n.)

One who is skilled in the art of naming loaves.

Breckles (n.)

A disease of artificial plants.

Brecon (n.)

The part of the toenail which is designed to snag on nylon sheets.

Brindle (vb.)

To remember suddenly where it is you're meant to be going after you've already been driving for ten minutes.

Brisbane (n.)

A perfectly reasonable explanation. (Such as one offered by a person with a gurgling cough which has nothing to do with the fact that they smoke fifty cigarettes a day.)

Brithdir (n.)

(Old Norse) The first day of the winter on which your breath condenses in the air.

Broats (pl.n.)

A pair of trousers with a career behind them. Broats are most commonly seen on elderly retired army officers. Originally the broats were part of their best suit back in the thirties; then in the fifties they were demoted and used for gardening. Recently, pensions not being what they were, the broats have been called out of retirement and reinstated as part of the best suit again.

Brompton (n.)

A brompton is that which is said to have been committed when you are convinced you are about to blow off with a resounding trumpeting noise in a public place and all that actually slips out is a tiny 'pfpt'.

Bromsgrove (n.)

Any urban environment containing a small amount of dog turd and about forty-five tons of bent steel pylon or a lump of concrete with holes claiming to be sculpture.

> Oh, come my dear, and come with me
> And wander 'neath the bromsgrove tree – Betjeman

Brough Sowerby (n.)

One who has been working at the same desk in the same office for fifteen years and has very much his own ideas about why he is continually passed over for promotion.

Brumby (n.)

The fake antique plastic seal on a pretentious whisky bottle.

Brymbo (n.)

The single unappetizing bun left in a baker's shop after four p.m.

Budby (n.)

A nipple clearly defined through flimsy or wet material.

Bude (n.)

A polite joke reserved for use in the presence of vicars.

Budle (vb.)

To fart underwater.

Buldoo (n.)

A virulent red-coloured pus which generally accompanies clonmult (q.v.) and sadberge (q.v.).

Burbage (n.)

The sound made by a liftful of people all trying to breathe through their noses.

Bures (pl.n.)

(Medical) The scabs on the knees and elbows formed by a compulsion to make love on cheap floor-matting.

Burleston (n.)

That peculiarly tuneless humming and whistling adopted by people who are extremely angry.

Burlingjobb (n.)

(Archaic) A seventeenth-century crime by which excrement is thrown into the street from a ground-floor window.

Burnt Yates (pl.n.)

Condition to which yates (q.v.) will suddenly pass without any apparent intervening period, after the spirit of the throckmorton (q.v.) has finally been summoned by incessant throcking (q.v.).

Bursledon (n.)

The bluebottle one is too tired to get up and swat, but not tired enough to sleep through.

Burslem (n.)

One who goes on talking at three o'clock in the morning after everyone else has gone to sleep. The principal habitat of burslems is Radio 2.

Burton Coggles (pl.n.)

The bunch of keys found in a drawer whose purpose has long been forgotten, and which can therefore now be used only for dropping down people's backs as a cure for nose-bleeds.

Burwash (n.)

The pleasurable cool sloosh of puddle water over the toes of your gumboots.

C

Caarnduncan (n.)

The high-pitched and insistent cry of the young male human urging one of its peer group to do something dangerous on a cliff-edge or piece of toxic waste ground.

Cadomin (n.)

The ingredient in coffee creamer that rises to the surface as scum.

Cafu (n.)

The frustration of not being able to remember what an acronym stands for.

Cahors (pl.n.)

The rushes of emotion triggered by overheard snatches of an old song.

Cairo (n.)

The noise of a spinning hub cap coming to rest.

Calicut (adj.)

Determined not to let someone see how much their inadvertent remark has hurt you.

Camer (n.)

A mis-tossed caber.

Cannock Chase (n.)

In any box of After Eight Mints, there is always a large number of empty envelopes and no more than four or five actual mints. The cannock chase is the process by which, no matter which part of the box you insert your fingers into, or how often, you will always extract most of the empty sachets before pinning down an actual mint, or 'cannock'.

The cannock chase also occurs with people who put dead matches back in the matchbox, and then embarrass themselves at parties trying to light cigarettes with three quarters of an inch of charcoal.

The term is also used to describe futile attempts to pursue unscrupulous advertising agencies who nick your ideas to sell chocolates with.

Canudos (n.)

The desire of married couples to see their single friends pair off.

Chaling (ptcpl.vb.)

Trying not to be driven up the wall by the opinions of someone whom circumstances will not allow you to argue with.

Cheb (n.)

An embarrassing nickname by which a fourteen-year-old boy insists that he now wishes to be known.

Chenies (pl.n.)

The last few sprigs or tassels of last year's Christmas decorations you notice on the ceiling while lying on the sofa on an August afternoon.

Chicago (n.)

The foul-smelling wind which precedes an underground train.

Chimbote (n.)

A newly fashionable ethnic stew which, however much everyone raves about it, seems to you to have rather a lot of fish-heads in it.

Chimkent (n.)

One whose life appears not to have moved on in any direction at all when you meet them again ten years later.

Chipping Ongar (n.)

The disgust and embarrassment (or 'ongar') felt by an observer in the presence of a person festooned with kirbies (q.v.), when they don't know them well enough to tell them to wipe them off. Invariably this 'ongar' is accompanied by an involuntary staccato twitching of the leg (or 'chipping').

Clabby (adj.)

A 'clabby' conversation is one struck up by a commissionaire or cleaning lady in order to avoid any further actual work. The opening gambit is usually designed to provoke the maximum confusion, and therefore the

longest possible clabby conversation. It is vitally important to learn the correct use of 'clixby' (q.v.), the response
to a clabby gambit, and not to get trapped by a 'ditherington' (q.v.). For instance, if confronted by a clabby
gambit such as 'Oh Mr Smith, I didn't know you'd had
your leg off', the ditherington response is 'I haven't . . .'
whereas the clixby is 'Good'.

Clackavoid (n.)

The technical term for a single page of script from an
Australian soap opera.

Clackmannan (n.)

The sound made by knocking over an elephant's-foot
umbrella-stand full of walking-sticks.

Clathy (adj.)

Nervously indecisive about how to dispose of a dud
lightbulb.

Clenchwarton (n.)

(Archaic) One who assists an exorcist by squeezing which-
ever part of the possessed the exorcist deems useful.

Climpy (adj.)

Allowing yourself to be persuaded to do something and
pretending to be reluctant.

Clingman's Dome (n.)

The condition in which it becomes impossible to put on a
tie correctly when in a hurry for an important meeting.

Clixby (adj.)

Politely rude. Briskly vague. Firmly uninformative.

Cloates Point (n.)

The precise instant at which scrambled eggs are ready.

Clonmult (n.)

A yellow ooze usually found near secretions of buldoo
(q.v.) and sadberge (q.v.).

Clovis (n.)

One who actually looks forward to putting up the Christmas decorations in the office.

Clun (n.)

A leg which has gone to sleep and has to be hauled around after you.

Clunes (pl.n.)

People who just won't go.

Coilantogle (n.)

(Vulg.) Long elasticated loop of snot which connects a pulled bogey to a nose.

Condover (n.)

One who is employed to stand about all day browsing through the magazine rack in the newsagent.

Cong (n.)

Strange-shaped metal utensil found at the back of the saucepan cupboard. Many authorities believe that congs provide conclusive proof of the existence of a now extinct form of yellow vegetable which the Victorians used to boil mercilessly.

CONG

Coodardy (adj.)

Astounded at what you've just managed to get away with.

Corfe (n.)

An object which is almost totally indistinguishable from a newspaper, the one crucial difference being that it belongs to somebody else and is unaccountably more interesting than your own – which may otherwise appear to be in all respects identical.

Though it is a rule of life that a train or other public place may contain any number of corfes but only one newspaper, it is quite possible to transform your own perfectly ordinary newspaper into a corfe by the simple expedient of letting someone else read it.

Corfu (n.)

The dullest person you met during the course of your holiday. Also the only one who failed to understand that the exchanging of addresses at the end of the holiday is merely a social ritual and is absolutely not an invitation to phone you up or turn up unannounced on your doorstep three months later.

Corriearklet (n.)

The moment at which two people, approaching from opposite ends of a long passageway, recognize each other and immediately pretend they haven't. This is to avoid the ghastly embarrassment of having to continue recognizing each other the whole length of the corridor.

Corriecravie (n.)

To avert the horrors of corrievorrie (q.v.), corriecravie is usually employed. This is the cowardly but highly skilled process by which both protagonists continue to approach while keeping up the pretence that they haven't noticed each other – by staring furiously at their feet, grimacing into a notebook, or studying the walls closely as if in a mood of deep irritation.

Corriedoo (n.)

The crucial moment of false recognition in a long passageway encounter. Though both people are perfectly well aware that the other is approaching, they must eventually pretend sudden recognition. They now look up with a glassy smile, as if having spotted each other for the first time, (and are particularly delighted to have done so), shouting out 'Haaaaalllllloooo!' as if to say 'Good grief!! You!! Here!! Of all people! Well I never. Coo. Stap me vitals,' etcetera.

Corriemoillie (n.)

The dreadful sinking sensation in a long passageway encounter when both protagonists immediately realize they have plumped for the corriedoo (q.v.) much too early as they are still a good thirty yards apart. They were embarrassed by the pretence of corriecravie (q.v.) and decided to make use of the corriedoo because they felt silly. This was a mistake as corrievorrie (q.v.) will make them seem far sillier.

Corriemuchloch (n.)

The kind of person who can make a complete mess of a simple job like walking down a corridor.

Corrievorrie (n.)

Corridor etiquette demands that once a corriedoo (q.v.) has been declared, corrievorrie must be employed. Both protagonists must now embellish their approach with an embarrassing combination of waving, grinning, making idiot faces, doing pirate impressions, and waggling the head from side to side while holding the other person's eyes as the smile drips off their face, until, with great relief, they pass each other.

Corstorphine (n.)

A very short peremptory service held in monasteries prior to tea-time to offer thanks for the benediction of digestive biscuits.

Cotterstock (n.)

A piece of wood used to stir paint and thereafter stored uselessly in the shed in perpetuity.

Cowcaddens (pl.n.)

A set of twelve cowcaddens makes an ideal and completely baffling wedding gift.

Craboon (vb.)

To shout boisterously from a cliff.

Crail (n.mineral)

Crail is a common kind of rock or gravel found widely across the British Isles.

Each individual stone (due to an as yet undiscovered gravitational property) is charged with 'negative buoyancy'. This means that no matter how much crail you remove from the garden, more of it will rise to the surface.

Crail is much employed by the Royal Navy for making the paperweights and ashtrays used in submarines.

Cranleigh (n.)

A mood of irrational irritation with everyone and everything.

Cresbard (n.)

The light working lunch which Anne Hathaway used to make for her husband.

Crieff (vb.)

To agree sycophantically with a taxi-driver about immigration.

Cromarty (n.)

The brittle sludge which clings to the top of ketchup bottles and plastic tomatoes in nasty cafés.

D

Dalderby (n.)

A letter to the editor made meaningless because it refers to a previous letter you didn't read. (See A.H. Hedgehope, July 3rd.)

Dalfibble (vb.)

To spend large swathes of your life looking for car keys.

Dallow (adj.)

Perfectly content to stare at something for no particular reason.

Dalmilling (ptcpl.vb.)

Continually making small talk to someone who is trying to read a book.

Dalrymple (n.)

Dalrymples are the things you pay extra for on pieces of handmade craftwork – the rough edges, the paint smudges and the holes in the glazing.

Damnaglaur (n.)

A certain facial expression which actors are required to demonstrate their mastery of before they are allowed to play Macbeth.

Darenth (n.)

Measure = 0.0000176 mg.

Defined as that amount of margarine capable of covering one hundred slices of bread to the depth of one molecule. This is the legal maximum allowed in sandwich bars in Greater London.

Darvel (vb.)

To hold out hope for a better invitation until the last possible moment.

Dattuck (n.)

One who performs drum solos on his knees.

Deal (n.)

The gummy substance found between damp toes.

Dean Funes (pl.n.)

Things that clergymen opine on that are none of their damn business.

Delaware (n.)

The hideous stuff on the shelves of a rented house.

Des Moines (pl.n.)

The two little lines that come down from your nose.

Detchant (n.)

The part of the hymn (usually a few notes at the end of the verse) where the tune goes so high or low that you suddenly have to change pitch to accommodate it.

Deventer (n.)

A decision that's very hard to take because so little depends on it – like which way to walk round a park.

Dewlish (adj.)

(Of the hands and feet.) Prunelike after an overlong bath.

Didcot (n.)

The tiny oddly shaped bit of card which a ticket inspector cuts out of a ticket with his clipper for no apparent reason. It is a little-known fact that the confetti at Princess Margaret's wedding was made up of thousands of didcots collected by inspectors on the Royal Train.

Dillytop (n.)

The kind of bath plug which for some unaccountable reason is actually designed to sit on top of the hole rather than fit into it.

Dinder (vb.)

To nod thoughtfully while someone gives you a long and complex set of directions which you know you're never going to remember.

Dinsdale (n.)

One who always plays 'Chopsticks' on the piano.

Dipple (vb.)

To try to remove a sticky something from one hand with the other, thus causing it to get stuck to the other hand and eventually to anything else you try to remove it with.

Ditherington (n.)

Sudden access of panic experienced by one who realizes that he is being drawn inexorably into a clabby (q.v.) conversation, i.e. one he has no hope of enjoying, benefiting from or understanding.

Dobwalls (pl.n.)

The now hard-boiled bits of nastiness which have to be prised off crockery by hand after it has been through a dishwasher.

Dockery (n.)

Facetious behaviour adopted by an accused man in the mistaken belief that this will endear him to the judge.

Dogdyke (vb.)

Of dog owners, to adopt the absurd pretence that the animal shitting in the gutter is nothing to do with them.

Dolgellau (n.)

The clump, or cluster, of bored, quietly enraged, mildly

embarrassed men waiting for their wives to come out of a changing room in a dress shop.

Dorchester (n.)

Someone else's throaty cough which obscures the crucial part of the rather amusing remark you've just made.

Dorridge (n.)

Technical term for one of the very lame excuses written in very small print on the side of packets of food or washing powder to explain why there's hardly anything inside. Examples include 'Contents may have settled in transit' and 'To keep biscuits fresh they have been individually wrapped in silver paper and cellophane and separated with corrugated lining, a cardboard flap, and heavy industrial tyres.'

Draffan (n.)

An infuriating person who always manages to look much more dashing than anyone else by turning up unshaven and hungover at a formal party.

Drebley (n.)

Name for a shop which is supposed to be witty but is in fact wearisome, e.g. 'The Frock Exchange', 'Hair Apparent', etc.

Droitwich (n.)

A street dance. The two partners approach from opposite directions and try politely to get out of each other's way. They step to the left, step to the right, apologize, step to the left again, bump into each other and repeat as often as unnecessary.

Drumsna (n.)

The earthquake that occurs when a character in a cartoon runs into a wall.

Dubbo (n.)

The bruise or callus on the shoulder of someone who has been knighted unnecessarily often.

Dubuque (n.)

A look given by a superior person to someone who has arrived wearing the wrong sort of shoes.

Duddo (n.)

The most deformed potato in any given collection of potatoes.

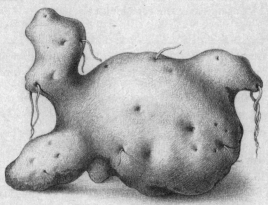

DUDDO

Dufton (n.)

The last page of a document that you always leave face down in the photocopier and have to go and retrieve later.

Duggleby (n.)

The person in front of you in the supermarket queue who has just unloaded a bulging trolley on to the conveyor belt and is now in the process of trying to work out which pocket they left their cheque book in, and indeed, which pair of trousers.

Duleek (n.)

Sudden realization, as you lie in bed waiting for the alarm to go off, that it should have gone off an hour ago.

Duluth (adj.)

The smell of a taxi out of which people have just got.

Dunbar (n.)

A highly specialized fiscal term used solely by turnstile operatives at Regent's Park zoo. It refers to the variable amount of increase in the gate takings on a Sunday afternoon, caused by persons going to the zoo because they are in love and believe that the feeling of romance will be somehow enhanced by the smell of panther sweat and rank incontinence in the reptile house.

Dunboyne (n.)

The realization that the train you have patiently watched pulling out of the station was the one you were meant to be on.

Duncraggon (n.)

The name of Charles Bronson's retirement cottage.

Dungeness (n.)

The uneasy feeling that the plastic handles of the overloaded supermarket carrier-bag you are carrying are getting steadily longer.

Dunino (n.)

Someone who always wants to do whatever you want to do.

Dunolly (n.)

An improvised umbrella.

Dunster (n.)

A small child hired to bounce at dawn on the occupants of the spare bedroom in order to save on tea and alarm clocks.

Duntish (adj.)

Mentally incapacitated by a severe hangover.

E

Eads (pl.n.)

The sludgy bits in the bottom of a dustbin, underneath the actual bin liner.

Eakring (ptcpl.vb.)

Wondering what to do next when you've just stormed out of something.

East Wittering (n.)

The same as West Wittering (q.v.), only it's you they're trying to get away from.

Edgbaston (n.)

The spare seat-cushion placed against the rear of a London bus to indicate that it has broken down.

Elgin (adj.)

Thin and haggard as a result of strenuously trying to get healthy.

Elsrickle (n.)

A bead of sweat which runs down your bottom cleavage.

Ely (n.)

The first, tiniest inkling that something, somewhere, has gone terribly wrong.

Emsworth (n.)

Measure of time and noiselessness defined as the moment between the doors of a lift closing and it beginning to move. Scientists believe we spend up to one fifth of our lives in lifts.

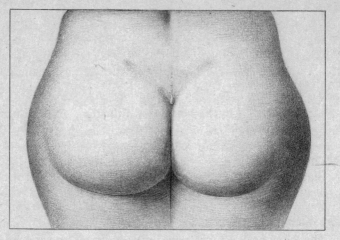

ELSRICKLE

Enumclaw (n.)
One of the initiation rituals of the Freemasons which they are no longer allowed to do.

Epping (ptcpl.vb.)
The futile movements of forefingers and eyebrows used when failing to attract the attention of waiters and barmen.

Epsom (n.)
An entry in a diary (such as a date or a set of initials) or a name and address in your address book, of which you haven't the faintest idea what it's doing there.

Epworth (n.)
The precise value of the usefulness of epping (q.v.). It is a little-known fact that an earlier draft of the final line of the film *Gone with the Wind* had Clark Gable saying 'Frankly, my dear, I don't give an epworth', the line being eventually changed on the grounds that it might not be understood in Iowa, or indeed anywhere.

Eriboll (n.)

A brown bubble of cheese containing gaseous matter which grows on welsh rarebit. It was Sir Alexander Fleming's study of eribolls which led, indirectly, to his discovery of the fact that he didn't like welsh rarebit much.

Esher (n.)

One of those push taps installed in public washrooms enabling the user to wash their trousers without actually getting into the basin. The most powerful esher of recent years was 'damped down' by Red Adair after an incredible sixty-eight days' fight in Manchester's Piccadilly Station.

Essendine (n.)

Long slow sigh emitted by a fake leather armchair when sat on.

Esterhazy (adj.)

(Medical term) Suffering from selective memory loss. The virus which causes this condition is thought to breed in the air-conditioning system of the White House.

Euphrates (n.)

The bullshit with which a chairman introduces a guest speaker.

Ewelme (n.)

The smile bestowed on you by an air hostess.

Exeter (n.)

All light household and electrical goods contain a number of vital components plus at least one exeter.

If you've just mended a fuse, changed a bulb or fixed a blender, the exeter is the small plastic piece left over which means you have to undo everything and start all over again.

F

Falster (n.)

A long-winded, dishonest and completely incredible excuse used when the truth would have been completely acceptable.

Famagusta (n.)

The draught which whistles between two bottoms that refuse to touch.

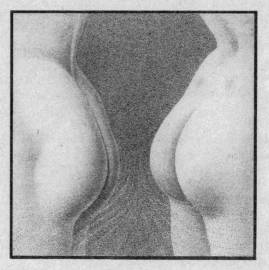

FAMAGUSTA

Farduckmanton (n.)

(Archaic) An ancient edict, mysteriously omitted from the Domesday Book, requiring that the feeding of fowl on village ponds should be carried out equitably.

Farnham (n.)

The feeling that you get at about four o'clock in the afternoon when you haven't got enough done.

Farrancassidy (n.)

A long and ultimately unsuccessful attempt to undo someone's bra.

Fentonadle (vb.)

To lay place settings with the knives and forks the wrong way round.

Ferfer (n.)

One who is very excited that they've had a better idea than the one you've just suggested.

Finuge (vb.)

In any division of foodstuffs equally between several people, to give yourself the extra slice left over.

Firebag (n.)

A remark intended to cue applause at a Tory party conference.

Fiunary (n.)

The safe place you put something and forget where it was.

Fladderbister (n.)

That part of a raincoat which trails out of a car after you've closed the door on it.

Flagler (n.)

Someone who always seems to disappear into shops when you're walking along talking to them.

Flimby (n.)

One of those irritating handle-less slippery translucent bags you get in supermarkets which, no matter how you hold them, always contrive to let something fall out.

Flodigarry (n.)

(Scots) An ankle-length oilskin worn by deep-sea fishermen in Arbroath and publicans in Glasgow.

Flums (pl.n.)

Women who only talk to each other at parties.

Foffarty (adj.)

Unable to find the right moment to leave.

Foindle (vb.)

To queue-jump very discreetly by working one's way up the line without being spotted doing so.

Foping (ptcpl.vb.)

Refusing to say what it is you're looking so bloody wistful about.

Forsinain (n.)

(Archaic) The right of the lord of the manor to molest dwarfs on their birthdays.

Fovant (n.)

A taxi-driver's gesture, a raised hand pointed out of the window which purports to mean 'thank you' but actually means 'bugger off out of my way'.

Fraddam (n.)

The small awkward-shaped piece of cheese which remains after grating a large regular-shaped piece of cheese, and which enables you to grate your fingers.

Framlingham (n.)

A kind of burglar alarm in common usage. It is cunningly designed so that it can ring at full volume in the street without apparently disturbing anyone.

Other types of framlinghams are burglar alarms fitted to business premises in residential areas, which go off as a matter of regular routine at 5.31 p.m. on a Friday evening and do not get turned off till 9.20 a.m. on Monday morning.

Frant (n.)

Measure. The legal minimum distance between two trains on the District and Circle lines of the London Underground. A frant, which must be not less than 122 chains (or 8 leagues) long, is not connected in any way with the adjective 'frantic' which comes to us by a completely different route (as indeed do the trains).

Frating Green (adj.)

The shade of green which is supposed to make you feel comfortable in hospitals, industrious in schools and uneasy in police stations.

Fremantle (vb.)

To steal things not worth the bother of stealing. One steals cars, money and silver. Book matches, airline eye-patches and individual pots of Trust House Forte apricot jam are merely fremantled.

Frimley (n.)

Exaggerated carefree saunter adopted by Norman Wisdom as an immediate prelude to dropping down an open manhole.

Fring (n.)

The noise made by a lightbulb that has just shone its last.

Fritham (n.)

A paragraph that you get stuck on in a book. The more you read it, the less it means to you.

Frolesworth (n.)

Measure. The minimum time it is necessary to spend frowning in deep concentration at each picture in an art gallery in order that everyone else doesn't think you're a complete moron.

Frosses (pl.n.)

The lecherous looks exchanged between sixteen-year-olds at a party given by someone's parents.

Frutal (adj.)

Rather too eager to be cruel to be kind.

Fulking (ptcpl.vb.)

Pretending not to be in when the carol-singers come round.

G

Gaffney (n.)

Someone who deliberately misunderstands things for, he hopes, humorous effect.

Galashiels (pl.n)

A form of particularly long sparse sideburns which are part of the mandatory turnout of British Rail guards.

Gallipolli (adj.)

Of the behaviour of a bottom lip trying to spit out mouth-wash after an injection at the dentist. Hence, loose, floppy, useless.

'She went all gallipoli in his arms' – Noel Coward

Gammersgill (n.)

Embarrassed stammer you emit when a voice answers the phone and you realize that you haven't the faintest recollection of who it is you've just rung.

Garrow (n.)

Narrow wiggly furrow left after pulling a hair off a painted surface.

Gartness (n.)

The ability to say 'No, there's absolutely nothing the

matter, what could possibly be the matter? And anyway I don't want to discuss it,' without moving your lips.

Garvock (n.)

The action of putting your finger in your cheek and flicking it out with a 'pock' noise.

Gastard (n.)

Useful specially new-coined word for an illegitimate child (in order to distinguish it from someone who merely carves you up on the motorway, etc.).

Ghent (adj.)

Descriptive of the mood indicated by cartoonists by drawing a character's mouth as a wavy line.

Gignog (n.)

Someone who, through the injudicious application of alcohol, is now a great deal less funny than he thinks he is.

Gildersome (adj.)

Descriptive of a joke someone tells you which starts well, but which becomes so embellished in the telling that you start to weary of it after scarcely half an hour.

Gilgit (n.)

Hidden sharply pointed object which stabs you in the cuticle when you reach into a small pot.

Gilling (n.)

The warm tingling you get in your feet when having a really good widdle.

Gipping (ptcpl.vb.)

The fish-like opening and closing of the jaws seen amongst people who have recently been to the dentist and are puzzled as to whether their teeth have been put back the right way up.

Glasgow (n.)

The feeling of infinite sadness engendered when walking

through a place filled with happy people fifteen years younger than yourself. When experienced too frequently, it is likely to lead to an attack of trunch (q.v.).

Glassel (n.)

A seaside pebble which was shiny and interesting when wet, and which is now a lump of rock, which children nevertheless insist on filling their suitcases with after the holiday.

Glazeley (adj.)

The state of a barrister's flat greasy hair after wearing a wig all day.

Glemanuilt (n.)

The kind of guilt which you'd completely forgotten about which comes roaring back on discovering an old letter in a cupboard.

Glenduckie (n.)

Any Scottish actor who wears a cravat.

Glentaggart (n.)

A particular type of tartan hold-all, made exclusively under licence for British Airways.

When waiting to collect your luggage from an airport conveyor belt, you will notice that on the next conveyor belt along there is always a single, solitary bag going round and round uncollected. This is a glentaggart, which has been placed there by the baggage-handling staff to take your mind off the fact that your own luggage will shortly be landing in Murmansk.

Glenties (pl.n.)

Series of small steps by which someone who has made a serious tactical error in conversation or argument moves from complete disagreement to wholehearted agreement.

Glenwhilly (n.)

    (Scots) A small tartan pouch worn beneath the kilt during the thistle-harvest.

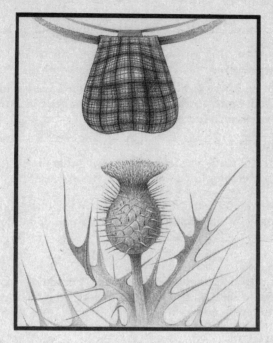

GLENWHILLY

Glinsk (n.)

    A hat which politicians buy to go to Russia in.

Glororum (n.)

    One who takes pleasure in informing others about their bowel movements.

Glossop (n.)

    A rogue blob of food.

    Glossops, which are generally steaming hot and highly adhesive, invariably fall off your spoon and on to the surface of your host's highly polished antique rosewood dining table. If this has not, or may not have, been noticed by the company present, swanage (q.v.) may be employed.

Glud (n.)

The pinkish mulch found in the bottom of a lady's handbag.

Glutt Lodge (n.)

The place where food can be stored after having a tooth extracted. Some Arabs can go without sustenance for up to six weeks on a full glutt lodge.

Godalming (n.)

Wonderful rush of relief on discovering that the ely (q.v.) and the wembley (q.v.) were in fact false alarms.

Goginan (n.)

The piece of elastoplast on a short-sighted child's spectacles.

Golant (adj.)

Blank, sly and faintly embarrassed. Pertaining to the expression seen on the face of someone who has clearly forgotten your name.

Gonnabarn (n.)

An afternoon wasted on watching an old movie on TV.

Goole (n.)

The puddle on the bar into which the barman puts your change.

Goosecruives (pl.n.)

(Archaic) A pair of wooden trousers worn by poultry-keepers in the Middle Ages.

Goosnargh (n.)

Something left over from preparing or eating a meal, which you store in the fridge despite the fact that you know full well that you will never ever use it.

Great Tosson (n.)

A fat book containing four words and six cartoons which costs £12.95.

Great Wakering (ptcpl.vb.)

Panic which sets in when you badly need to go to the lavatory and cannot make up your mind about what book or magazine to take with you.

Greeley (n.)

Someone who continually annoys you by continually apologizing for annoying you.

Gress (vb.)

(Rare) To stick to the point during a family argument.

Gretna Green (adj.)

A shade of green which makes you wish you'd painted whatever it was a different colour.

Gribun (n.)

The person in a crisis who can always be relied on to make a good anecdote out of it.

Grimbister (n.)

Large body of cars on a motorway all travelling at exactly the speed limit because one of them is a police car.

Grimmet (n.)

A small bush from which cartoon characters dangle over the edge of a cliff.

Grimsby (n.)

A lump of something gristly and foul-tasting concealed in a mouthful of stew or pie.

Grimsbies are sometimes merely the result of careless cookery, but more often they are placed there deliberately by Freemasons. Grimsbies can be purchased in bulk from any respectable Masonic butcher on giving him the secret Masonic handbag. One is then placed in a guest's food to see if he knows the correct Masonic method of dealing with it.

This is as follows: remove the grimsby carefully with the silver tongs provided. Cross the room to your host, hopping on one leg, and ram the grimsby firmly up his nose, chanting, 'Take that, you smug Masonic bastard.'

Grinstead (n.)

The state of a woman's clothing after she has been to powder her nose and has hitched up her tights over her skirt at the back, thus exposing her bottom, and has walked out without noticing it.

Grobister (n.)

One who continually and publicly rearranges the position of his genitals.

Gruids (n.)

The only bits of an animal left after even the people who make sausage rolls have been at it.

Grutness (n.)

The resolve with which the Queen sits through five days of Polynesian folk dancing.

Gubblecote (n.)

Deformation of the palate caused by biting into too many Toblerones.

Guernsey (adj.)

Queasy but unbowed. The kind of feeling one gets when discovering a plastic compartment in a fridge in which things are growing, usually fertilized by copious quantities of goosnargh (q.v.).

Gulberwick (n.)

The small particle that you always think you've got stuck in the back of your throat after you've been sick.

Gussage (n.)

Dress-making talk.

Gweek (n.)

A coat hanger recycled as a car aerial.

H

Hadweenzic (adj.)

Resistant to tweezers.

Hadzor (n.)

A sharp instrument placed in the washing-up bowl which makes it easier to cut yourself.

Hagnaby (n.)

Someone who looked a lot more attractive in the disco than they do in your bed the next morning.

Halcro (n.)

An adhesive cloth designed to fasten baby-clothes together. Thousands of tiny pieces of jam 'hook' on to thousands of pieces of dribble, enabling the cloth to become 'sticky'.

Halifax (n.)

The green synthetic astroturf on which greengrocers display their vegetables.

Hallspill (n.)

The name for the adventurous partygoers who don't spend the whole time in the kitchen.

Hambledon (n.)

The sound of a single-engined aircraft flying by, heard while lying in a summer field in England, which somehow concentrates the silence and sense of space and timelessness and leaves one with the feeling of something or other.

Hankate (adj.)

Congenitally incapable of ever having a paper tissue.

Happas (n.)

The amusement caused by passport photos.

Happle (vb.)

To annoy people by finishing their sentences for them and then telling them what they really meant to say.

Harbledown (vb.)

To manoeuvre a double mattress down a winding staircase.

Harbottle (n.)

A particular kind of fly which lives inside double glazing.

Harlosh (vb.)

To redistribute the hot water in a bath.

Harmanger (n.)

The person who takes the blame while the manager you demanded to see hides in his office.

Harpenden (n.)

The coda to a phone conversation, consisting of about eight exchanges, by which people try gracefully to get off the line.

Haselbury Plucknett (n.)

A mechanical device for cleaning combs invented during the industrial revolution at the same time at Arkwright's Spinning Jenny, but which didn't catch on in the same way.

Hassop (n.)

The pocket down the back of an armchair used for storing 10p pieces and bits of Lego.

Hastings (pl.n.)

Things said on the spur of the moment to explain to

someone who unexpectedly comes into a room, precisely what it is you are doing.

Hathersage (n.)

The tiny snippets of beard which coat the inside of a washbasin after shaving in it.

Haugham (n.)

One who loudly informs other diners in a restaurant what kind of man he is by calling the chef by his Christian name from the lobby.

Haxby (n.)

Any gardening implement found in a potting-shed whose exact purpose is unclear.

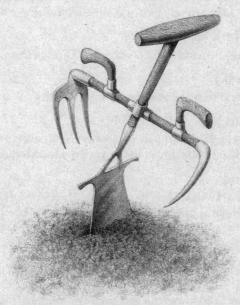

HAXBY

Heanton Punchardon (n.)

A violent argument which breaks out in the car on the

way home from a party between a couple who have had to be polite to each other in company all evening.

Henstridge (n.)

A dried yellow substance found between the prongs of forks in restaurants.

Hepple (vb.)

To sculpt the contents of a sugar bowl.

Herstmonceux (n.)

The correct name for the gold medallion worn by someone who is in the habit of wearing their shirt open to the waist.

Hessle (vb.)

To try and sort out which sleeve of a sweater is inside out when you're already half-way through putting it on.

Hever (n.)

The panic caused by half-hearing a Tannoy in an airport.

Hewish (adj.)

In a mood to swipe at vegetation with a stick.

Hextable (n.)

The record you find in someone else's collection which instantly tells you you could never go out with them.

Hibbing (n.)

The marks left on the outside breast pocket of a storekeeper's overall where he put away his pen and missed.

Hickling (ptcpl.vb.)

The practice of infuriating theatre-goers by not only arriving late to a centre-row seat, but also loudly apologizing to and patting each member of the audience in turn.

Hidcote Bartram (n.)

To be caught in a hidcote bartram is to say a series of

protracted and final goodbyes to a group of people and then realize that you've left your hat behind.

High Limerigg (n.)

The topmost tread of a staircase which disappears when you're climbing the stairs in darkness.

High Offley (n.)

Goosnargh (q.v.) three weeks later.

Hobarris (n.)

(Medical) A sperm which carries a high risk of becoming a bank manager.

Hobbs Cross (n.)

The awkward leaping manoeuvre a girl has to go through in bed in order to make him sleep on the wet patch.

Hoddlesdon (n.)

An 'injured' footballer's limp back into the game which draws applause but doesn't fool anybody.

Hodnet (n.)

The wooden safety platform supported by scaffolding round a building under construction from which the builders (at almost no personal risk) can drop pieces of concrete on passers-by.

Hoff (vb.)

To deny indignantly something which is palpably true.

Hoggeston (n.)

The action of overshaking a pair of dice in a cup in the mistaken belief that this will affect the eventual outcome in your favour and not irritate everyone else.

Hordle (vb.)

To dissemble in a fruity manner, like Donald Sinden.

Horton-cum-Studley (n.)

The combination of little helpful grunts, nodding movements of the head, considerate smiles, upward frowns and serious pauses that a group of people join in making to elicit the next pronouncement of somebody with a terrible stutter.

Hosmer (vb.)

(Of a TV newsreader) To continue to stare impassively into the camera when it should have already switched to the sports report.

Hotagen (n.)

The aggressiveness with which a shop assistant sells you any piece of high technology which they don't understand themselves.

Hove (adj.)

Descriptive of the expression on the face of a person in the presence of another who clearly isn't going to stop talking for a very long time.

Huby (n.)

A half-erection large enough to be a publicly embarrassing bulge in the trousers, but not large enough to be of any use to anybody.

Hucknall (vb.)

To crouch upwards: as in the movement of a seated person's feet and legs made to allow a cleaner's Hoover to pass beneath them.

Hugglescote (n.)

The kind of person who excitedly opens a letter which says 'You may already have won £10,000' on the outside.

Hull (adj.)

Descriptive of the smell of a weekend cottage.

Humber (vb.)

To move like the cheeks of a very fat person as their car goes over a cattle grid.

Humby (n.)

An erection which won't go down when a gentleman has to go to the lavatory in the middle of dallying with a lady.

Huna (n.)

The result of coming to the wrong decision.

Hunsingore (n.)

Medieval ceremonial brass horn with which the successful execution of an araglin (q.v.) is trumpeted from the castle battlements.

Hutlerburn (n.)

(Archaic) A burn sustained as a result of the behaviour of a clumsy hutler. (The precise duties of hutlers are now lost in the mists of history.)

Huttoft (n.)

The fibrous algae which grow in the dark, moist environment of trouser turn-ups.

Hynish (adj.)

Descriptive of the state of mind in which you might as well give up doing whatever it is you're trying to do because you'll only muck it up.

I

Ible (adj.)

Clever but lazy.

Ibstock (n.)

Anything used to make a noise on a corrugated iron wall or clinker-built fence by dragging it along the surface while walking past it.

'Mr Bennett thoughtfully selected a stout ibstock and left the house.' – Jane Austen, *Pride and Prejudice*, II.

Imber (vb.)

To lean from side to side while watching a car chase in the cinema.

Inigonish (adj.)

Descriptive of the expression on a dinner party guest which is meant to indicate huge enjoyment to the hosts and 'time to go home I think' to your partner. An inigonish is usually the prelude to a heanton puncharddon (q.v.).

Inverinate (vb.)

To spot that both people in a heated argument are talking complete rubbish.

Inverkeithing (ptcpl.vb.)

Addressing someone by mumble because you can only remember the first letter of their name.

Iping (ptcpl.vb.)

The increasingly anxious shifting from leg to leg you go through when you are desperate to go to the lavatory and the person you are talking to keeps on remembering a few final things he wants to mention.

Ipplepen (n.)

A useless writing implement made by Sellotaping six biros together which is supposed to make it easier to write 100 lines.

Ipswich (n.)

The sound at the other end of the telephone which tells you that the automatic exchange is working very hard but is intending not actually to connect you this time, merely to let you know how difficult it is.

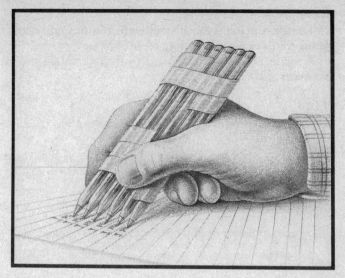

IPPLEPEN

Islesteps (pl.n.)

Cautious movements towards the bathroom in a strange house in the dark.

J

Jalingo (n.)

The alacrity with which a grimbister (q.v.) breaks up as soon as the police car turns off.

Jarrow (n.)

An agricultural device which, when towed behind a tractor, enables the farmer to spread his dung evenly across the width of the road.

Jawcraig (n.)

(Medical) A massive facial spasm which is brought on by being told a really astounding piece of news.

A mysterious attack of jawcraig affected 40,000 sheep in Wales in 1952.

Jawf (n.)

Conversation between two football hooligans on a train.

Jeffers (pl.n.)

Persons who honestly believe that a business lunch is going to achieve something.

Jid (n.)

The piece of paper on top of the jam inside the jam jar.

Jofane (adj.)

In breach of the laws of joke telling, e.g. giving away the punchline in advance.

Joliette (n.)

(Old French) Polite word for a well-proportioned dog-turd.

Joplin (n.)

The material from which all the clothes in Woolworths are made.

Jubones (pl.n.)

Awful things bought in Nairobi which never look good at home.

Jurby (n.)

A loose woollen garment reaching to the knees and with three or more armholes, knitted by the wearer's well-meaning but incompetent aunt.

Juwain (adj.)

Only slightly relevant to the matter in hand.

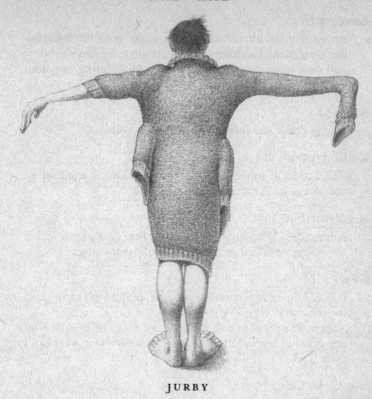

JURBY

K

Kabwum (n.)

The cutesy humming noise you make as you go to kiss someone on the cheek.

Kalami (n.)

The ancient Eastern art of being able to fold road maps properly.

55

Kanturk (n.)

An extremely intricate knot originally used for belaying the topgallant foresheets of a gaff-rigged China clipper, and now more commonly observed when trying to get an old kite out of the cupboard under the stairs.

Keele (n.)

The horrible smell caused by washing ashtrays.

Kelling (ptcpl.vb.)

The action of looking for something all over again in all the places you've already looked.

Kenilworth (n.)

A measure. Defined as that proportion of a menu which the waiter speaks that you can actually remember.

Kent (adj.)

Politely determined not to help despite a violent urge to the contrary.

Kent expressions are seen on the faces of people who are good at something watching someone else who can't do it at all.

Kentucky (adj.)

Fitting exactly and satisfyingly.

The cardboard box that slides neatly into a small space in a garage, or the last book which precisely fills a bookshelf, is said to fit 'real nice and kentucky'.

Kerry (n.)

The small twist of skin which separates each sausage on a string.

Kettering (n.)

The marks left on your bottom or thighs after sunbathing on a wickerwork chair.

Kettleness (adj.)

The quality of not being able to pee while being watched.

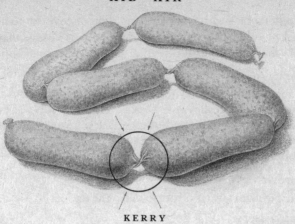

KERRY

Kibblesworth (n.)

The footling amount of money by which the price of a given article in a shop is less than a sensible number, in the hope that at least one idiot will think it cheap. For instance, the kibblesworth on a pair of shoes priced at £19.99 is 1p.

Kilvaxter (n.)

A pen kept in the desk tidy that never works.

Kimmeridge (n.)

The light breeze which blows through your armpit hair when you are stretched out sunbathing.

Kingston Bagpuise (n.)

A forty-year-old sixteen-stone man trying to commit suicide by jogging.

Kirby (n.)

Small but repulsive piece of food prominently attached to a person's face or clothing.

Kirby Misperton (n.)

One who kindly attempts to wipe a kirby (q.v.) off

another's face with a napkin, and then discovers it to be a wart or other permanent fixture, is said to have committed a 'kirby misperton'.

Kitmurvy (n.)

A man who owns all the latest sporting gadgetry and clothing (golf trolley, tee cosies, ventilated shoes, Sevvy Ballesteros autographed tracksuit top, American navy cap, mirror sunglasses) but is still only on his second golf lesson. -

Kittybrewster (n.)

The girl who always offers to make the tea.

Klosters (pl.n.)

The little blobs of dried urine on the rim of the bowl under the seat.

Knaptoft (n.)

The mysterious fluff placed in your pockets by dry-cleaning firms.

Kowloon (n.)

One who goes to an Indian restaurant and orders an omelette.

Kurdistan (n.)

Hard stare given by a husband to his wife when he notices a sharp increase in the number of times he answers the phone to be told, 'Sorry, wrong number.'

L

Lackawanna (n.)

The inability of a New York cab driver to know where, for instance, Central Park is.

Lambarene (adj.)

Feeling better for having put pyjamas on.

Lamlash (n.)

The folder on hotel dressing-tables full of astoundingly dull information.

Lampeter (n.)

The fifth member of a foursome.

Lampung (n.)

The daze which follows turning on the light in the middle of the night.

Largoward (n.)

Motorists' name for the kind of pedestrian who stands beside a main road and waves on the traffic, as if it's their right of way.

Laxobigging (ptcpl.vb.)

Struggling to extrude an extremely large turd.

Le Touquet (n.)

A mere nothing, an unconsidered trifle, a negligible amount. Un touquet is often defined as the difference between the cost of a bottle of gin bought in an off-licence shop and one bought in a duty-free shop.

Leazes (pl.n.)

Irritating pains that your doctor tells you not to be so wet about.

Leeming (ptcpl.vb.)

The business of making silly faces at babies.

Lemvig (n.)

A person who can be relied upon to be doing worse than you.

Libenge (n.)

Crystallized deposits of old cough mixture.

Libode (adj.)

Being undecided about whether or not you feel sexually attracted to someone.

Liff (n.)

A common object or experience for which no word yet exists.

Limassol (n.)

The correct name for one of those little paper umbrellas which come in cocktails with too much pineapple juice in them.

Lindisfarne (adj.)

Descriptive of the pleasant smell of an empty biscuit tin.

Lingle (vb.)

To touch battery terminals with one's tongue.

Liniclate (adj.)

All stiff and achey in the morning and trying to remember why.

Listowel (n.)

The small mat on the bar designed to be more absorbent than the bar, but not as absorbent as your elbows.

Little Urswick (n.)

The member of any class who most inclines the teacher towards the view that capital punishment should be introduced in schools.

Llanelli (adj.)

Descriptive of the waggling movement of a person's hands when shaking water from them or warming up for a piece of workshop theatre.

Loberia (n.)

Unshakeable belief that your ears stick out.

Lochranza (n.)

The long unaccompanied wail in the middle of a Scottish folk song where the pipers nip round the corner for a couple of drinks.

Lolland (n.)

A person with a low threshold of boredom.

Longniddry (n.)

A droplet which persists in running out of your nose.

Lossiemouth (n.)

One of those middle-aged ladies with just a hint of a luxuriant handlebar moustache.

Lostwithiel (n.)

The deep and peaceful sleep you finally fall into two minutes before the alarm goes off.

Louth (n.)

The sort of man who wears loud check jackets, has a personalized tankard behind the bar and always gets served before you do.

Low Ardwello (n.)

Seductive remark made hopefully in the back of a taxi.

Low Eggborough (n.)

A quiet little unregarded man in glasses who is building a new kind of atomic bomb in his garden shed.

Lower Peover (n.)

Common solution to the problem of a humby (q.v.).

Lowestoft (n.)

The correct name for 'navel fluff'.

Lowther (vb.)

(Of a large group of people who have been to the cinema together.) To stand aimlessly about on the pavement and argue about whether to go and eat either a Chinese meal nearby or an Indian meal at a restaurant which somebody says is very good but isn't certain where it is, or just go home, or have a Chinese meal nearby – until by the time agreement is reached everything is shut.

Lubcroy (n.)

The telltale little lump in the top of your swimming trunks which tells you you are going to have to spend half an hour with a safety pin trying to pull the drawstring out again.

Lublin (n.)

That bit of somebody's body which their partner particularly likes.

Ludlow (n.)

A wad of newspaper, folded table-napkin or lump of cardboard put under a wobbly table or chair to make it stand up straight.

It is perhaps not widely known that air-ace Sir Douglas Bader used to get about on an enormous pair of ludlows before he had his artificial legs fitted.

Luffenham (n.)

Feeling you get when the pubs aren't going to be open for another forty-five minutes and the luffness (q.v.) is beginning to wear a bit thin.

Luffness (n.)

Hearty feeling that comes from walking on the moors with gumboots and cold ears.

Lulworth (n.)

Measure of conversation.

A lulworth defines the amount of the length, loudness and embarrassment of a statement you make when everyone else in the room unaccountably stops talking at the same moment.

Luppitt (n.)

The piece of leather which hangs off the bottom of your shoe before you can be bothered to get it mended.

Lupridge (n.)

A bubble behind a piece of wallpaper.

Lusby (n.)

The fold of flesh pushing forward over the top of a bra which is too small for the lady inside it.

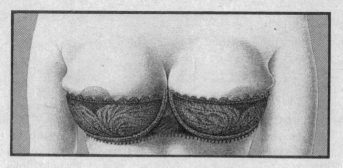

LUSBY

Luton (n.)

The horseshoe-shaped rug which goes round a lavatory seat.

Lutton Gowts (n.)

The opposite of green fingers – the effortless propensity to cause plant death.

Lybster (n.)

The artificial chuckle in the voice-over at the end of a supposedly funny television commercial.

Lydd (n.)

A lid. A lydd differs from a lid in that it has nothing to be a lid of, is at least eighteen months old, and is sold in Ye Olde Antique Shoppes.

Lydiard Tregoze (n.)

The opposite of a mavis enderby (q.v.). An unrequited early love of your life who inexplicably still causes terrible pangs even though she married a telephone engineer. .

Lyminster (n.)

A homosexual vicar.

Lynwilg (n.)

One of those things that pulls the electric cord back into a vacuum cleaner.

M

Maaruig (n.)

The inexpressible horror experienced on waking up in the morning and remembering that you are Andy Stewart.

Macroy (n.)

An authoritative, confident opinion based on one you read in a newspaper.

Malaybalay (adj.)

All excited at suddenly remembering a wonderful piece of gossip that you want to pass on to somebody.

Malibu (n.)

The height by which the top of a wave exceeds the height to which you have rolled up your trousers.

Manitoba (n.)

A re-courtship ritual. The tentative and reluctant touching of spouses' toes in bed after a row.

Mankinholes (pl.n.)

The small holes in a loaf of bread which give rise to the

momentary suspicion that something may have made its home within.

MALIBU

Mapledurham (n.)

A hideous piece of chipboard veneer furniture bought in a suburban high-street furniture store and designed to hold exactly a year's supply of Sunday colour supplements.

Margaretting Tye (n.)

The unexpectedly intimate bond that forms when two people you have just introduced decide they like each other better than they like you.

Margate (n.)

A margate is a particular kind of commissionaire who sees you every day and is on cheerful Christian-name terms with you, then one day refuses to let you in because you've forgotten your identity card.

Market Deeping (ptcpl.vb.)

Stealing a single piece of fruit from a street stall.

Marlow (n.)

The bottom drawer in the kitchen where your mother keeps her paper bags.

Marytavy (n.)
A person to whom, under dire injunctions of silence, you tell a secret which you wish to be far more widely known.

Masberry (n.)
The sap of a giant Nigerian tree from which all canteen jams are made.

Massachusetts (pl.n.)
Those items and particles which people who have just blown their noses are searching for when they look into their hankies.

Mavesyn Ridware (n.)
The stuff belonging to a mavis enderby (q.v.) which keeps turning up in odd corners of your house.

Mavis Enderby (n.)
The almost-completely-forgotten girlfriend from your distant past for whom your wife has a completely irrational jealousy and hatred.

Maynooth (n.)
One who recklessly tells total strangers to cheer up, it may never happen.

Meadle (vb.)
To blunder around a woman's breasts in a way which does absolutely nothing for her.

Meath (adj.)
Warm and very slightly clammy.
    Descriptive of the texture of your hands after you've tried to dry them on a hot-air-blowing automatic hand-drying machine.

Melbury Bubb (n.)
A TV celebrity who rises to fame by being extremely camp.

Melcombe Regis (n.)
The name of the style of decoration used in cocktail lounges in mock-Tudor hotels in Surrey.

Melton Constable (n.)

A patent anti-wrinkle cream which policemen wear to keep themselves looking young.

Memphis (n.)

The little bits of yellow fluff which get trapped in the hinge of the windscreen wipers after polishing the car with a new duster.

Memus (n.)

The little trick people use to remind themselves which is left and which is right.

Meuse (n.)

A period of complete silence on the radio, which means that it must be tuned to Radio 3.

Millinocket (n.)

The thing that rattles around inside an aerosol can.

Milwaukee (n.)

The melodious whistling, chanting and humming tone of the milwaukee can be heard whenever a public lavatory is entered. It is the way the occupants of the cubicles have of telling you there's no lock on their door and you can't come in.

Mimbridge (n.)

That which two very boring people have in common which enables you to get away from them.

Minchinhampton (n.)

The expression on a man's face when he has just zipped his trousers up without due care and attention.

Misool (n.)

A mixture of toothpaste and saliva in a wash-basin.

Moffat (n.)

That part of a coat which is designed to be sat on by the person next to you on the bus.

Mogumber (n.)

One who goes round complaining they were cleverer ten years ago.

Mointy (n.)

The last little tear before somebody cheers up.

Moisie (adj.)

The condition of one's face after performing cunnilingus.

Molesby (n.)

The kind of family that drives to the seaside and then sits in the car with all the windows closed, reading the *Sunday Express* and wearing sidcups (q.v.).

Monks Toft (n.)

The bundle of hair which is left after a monk has been tonsured, which he keeps tied up with a rubber band and uses for chasing ants away.

Morangie (adj.)

Faintly nervous that a particular post box 'won't work' when posting an important letter.

Motspur (n.)

The fourth wheel of a supermarket trolley which looks identical to the other three but renders the trolley completely uncontrollable.

Mugeary (n.)

(Medical) The substance from which the unpleasant little yellow globules in the corners of a sleepy person's eyes are made.

Multan (n.)

An infidel who stains his face with walnut juice in order to enter Mecca or appear in a sitcom.

Mummelgum (n.)

An unwholesome substance which clings to the fingers of successful tomb-robbers.

Munderfield (n.)

A meadow selected, whilst driving past, as being ideal for a picnic which, from a sitting position, turns out to be full of stubble, dust and cowpats and almost impossible to enjoy yourself in.

Munster (n.)

A person who continually brings up the subject of property prices.

N

Naas (n.)

The winemaking region of Albania where most of the aasleagh (q.v.) comes from.

Nacton (n.)

The 'n' with which cheap advertising copywriters replace the word 'and' (as in 'fish 'n' chips', 'mix 'n' match', 'assault 'n' battery'), in the mistaken belief that it is in some way chummy or endearing.

Nad (n.)

Measure defined as the distance between a driver's outstretched fingertips and the ticket machine in an automatic car-park.
1 nad = 18.4 cm.

Namber (vb.)

To hang around the table being too shy to sit next to the person you really want to.

Nanhoron (n.)

A tiny valve concealed in the inner ear which enables a deaf grandmother to converse quite normally when she feels like it, but which excludes completely anything which sounds like a request to help with laying the table.

Nantucket (n.)
The secret pocket which eats your train ticket.

Nantwich (n.)
A late-night snack, invented by the Earl of Nantwich, which consists of the dampest thing in the fridge. The Earl, who lived in a flat in Clapham, invented the nantwich to avoid having to go shopping.

Naples (pl.n.)
The tiny depressions in a piece of Ryvita.

NAPLES

Naugatuck (n.)
A plastic sachet containing shampoo, polyfilla, etc., which is impossible to open except by biting off the corners.

Nazeing (ptcpl.vb.)
The rather unconvincing noises of pretended interest which an adult has to make when brought a small dull object for admiration by a child.

Neen Sollars (pl.n.)

Any ensemble of especially unflattering and peculiar garments worn by someone which tells you that they are right at the forefront of fashion.

Nempnett Thrubwell (n.)

The feeling experienced when driving off for the very first time on a brand new motorbike.

Nindigully (n.)

One who constantly needs to be re-persuaded of something they've already agreed to.

Nipishish (adj.)

Descriptive of a person walking barefoot on gravel.

Nith (n.)

The dark piece of velvet which has been brushed against the nap.

Noak Hoak (n.)

A driver who indicates left and turns right.

Nogdam End (n.)

That part of a pair of scissors used to bang in a picture hook.

Nokomis (n.)

One who dresses like an ethnic minority to which they do not belong.

Nome (sfx.)

Latin suffix meaning: question expecting the answer 'Oh really? How interesting.'

Nossob (n.)

Any word that looks as if it's probably another word backwards but turns out not to be.

Nottage (n.)

The collective name for things which you find a use for

immediately after you have thrown them away.

For instance, your greenhouse has been cluttered up for years with a huge piece of cardboard and great fronds of gardening string. You at last decide to clear all this stuff out, and you burn it. Within twenty-four hours you will urgently need to wrap a large parcel, and suddenly remember that luckily in your greenhouse there is some cardb . . .

Nubbock (n.)
The kind of person who has to leave before a party can relax and enjoy itself.

Nuncargate (adj.)
Able to go on a two-week holiday with hardly any luggage.

Nundle (vb.)
To move a piano.

Nupend (n.)
The amount of small change found in the lining of an old jacket which just saves your bacon.

Nutbourne (n.)
In a choice between two or more possible puddings, the one nobody plumps for.

Nyarling (ptcpl.vb.)
Of married couples, using a term of endearment as a term of censure or reproach.

Nybster (n.)
The sort of person who takes the lift to travel one floor.

O

Ocilla (n.)

The cute little circle or heart over an 'i' used by teenage girls when writing their names.

Ockle (n.)

An electrical switch which appears to be off in both positions.

Offleyhoo (adj.)

Ridiculously over-enthusiastic about going to Cornwall.

Offord Darcy (n.)

A gatecrasher you can't get rid of because he's become the life and soul of the party.

Old Cassop (n.)

Piece of caring reassurance which all parties know is completely untrue. As in 'a load of . . .'

Ompton (n.)

One who has been completely kitted out at Burberry's but is still, nevertheless, clearly from Idaho.

Osbaston (n.)

A point made for the seventh time to somebody who insists that they know exactly what you mean but clearly hasn't got the faintest idea.

Oshkosh (n.)

The noise made by someone who has just been grossly flattered and is trying to make light of it.

Ospringe (n.)

That part of a three-colour biro which renders it instantly useless.

Ossett (n.)

A frilly spare-toilet-roll cosy.

OSSETT

Ossining (ptcpl.vb.)

Trying to see past the person sitting in front of you at the cinema.

Oswaldtwistle (n.)

(Old Norse) Small brass wind instrument used for summoning Vikings to lunch when they're off on their longships, playing.

Oswestry (n.)

The inability to find a comfortable position to lie in bed.

Oughterby (n.)

Someone you don't want to invite to a party but whom you know you have to as a matter of duty.

Oundle (vb.)

To walk along leaning sideways, with one arm hanging limp and dragging one leg behind the other.

Most commonly used by actors in amateur productions of *Richard III*, or by people carrying a heavy suitcase in one hand.

Oystermouth (n.)

One who can kiss and chew gum at the same time.

Ozark (n.)

One who offers to help after all the work has been done.

P

Pabbay (n.)

(Fencing term.) The play, or manoeuvre, where one swordsman leaps on to the table and pulls the battleaxe off the wall.

Pant-y-Wacco (adj.)

The final state of mind of a retired colonel before they come to take him away.

Pantperthog (n.)

An actor whose only talent is to stay fat.

Papcastle (n.)

Something drawn or modelled by a small child which you are supposed to know what it is.

Papigochic (n.)

A middle-aged man's overlong haircut, intended to make him look younger.

Papple (vb.)

To do what babies do to soup with their spoons.

Papworth Everard (n.)

Technical term for the fifth take of an orgasm scene during the making of a pornographic film.

Paradip (n.)

Polite word for the act of washing one's genitals in the wash-basin.

Parbold (adj.)

Nearly brave enough to dive into a cold swimming pool on a windy day.

Parrog (n.)

God knows. Could be some sort of bird, I suppose.

Pathstruie (adj.)

The condition of a parish church after a heavy Saturday afternoon's wedlock.

Patkai Bum (n.)

Mysterious illness afflicting recently deposed heads of state which means they aren't well enough to stand trial.

Patney (n.)

Something your next door neighbour makes and insists that you try on your sausages.

Peebles (pl.n.)

Small, carefully rolled pellets of skegness (q.v.).

Peening Quarter (n.)

That area of a discotheque where single men lounge about trying to look groovy about not having the courage to ask a girl to dance.

Pelutho (n.)

A South American ball game. The balls are whacked

against a brick wall with a stout wooden bat until the prisoner confesses.

Pen tre-tafarn-y-fedw (n.)

Welsh word which literally translates as 'leaking-biro-by-the-glass-hole-of-the-clerk-of-the-bank-has-been-taken-to-another-place-leaving-only-the-special-inkwell-and-three-inches-of-tin-chain'.

Penge (n.)

The expanding slotted arm on which a cuckoo comes out of a cuckoo clock.

PENGE

Peoria (n.)

The fear of peeling too few potatoes.

Percyhorner (n.)

(English public-school slang) A prefect whose duty it is to surprise new boys at the urinal and humiliate them in a manner of his choosing.

Perranzabuloe (n.)

One of those spray things used to wet ironing with.

Peru (n.)

The expression of innocent alarm seen on the face of someone guiltily surprised in the middle of a perusal.

Peterculter (n.)

Someone you don't want to be friends with who rings you up at eight-monthly intervals and suggests you get together soon.

Pevensey (n.)

(Archaic) The right to collect shingle from the king's foreshore.

Phillack (n.)

A Gucci belt pouch for carrying condoms in.

Pibsbury (n.)

The little hole in the end of a toothbrush.

Picklenash (n.)

The detritus found in wine glasses on the morning after a party.

Piddletrenthide (n.)

A trouser stain caused by a wimbledon (q.v.). Not to be confused with a botley (q.v.).

Pidney (n.)

The amount of coffee in the bottom of the jar which doesn't amount to a spoonful.

Pimlico (n.)

Small odd-shaped piece of plastic or curious metal component found in the bottom of a kitchen rummage-drawer when spring-cleaning or looking for Sellotape.

Pimperne (n.)

One of those rubber nodules found on the underneath side of a lavatory seat.

Pingandy (n.)

An extremely neat old person.

Pingaring (n.)

That part of an oven that nobody wants or knows how to turn off.

Pitlochry (n.)

The background gurgling noise heard in fast food restaurants caused by people trying to get the last bubbles out of their milkshakes by slurping loudly through their straws.

Pitroddie (n.)

A middle- or upper-class person who affects a working-class style of speech.

Pitsligo (n.)

Part of traditional mating rite.

During the first hot day of spring, all the men in the tube start giving up their seats to ladies and straphanging. The purpose of pitsligo is to allow them to demonstrate their manhood by displaying the wet patches under their arms.

Pleeley (adj.)

Descriptive of a drunk person's attempts to be endearing.

Plenmeller (n.)

The non-waterproof material from which raincoats are made.

Pleven (n.)

One more, or one less, than the number required.

Plumgarths (pl.n)

The corrugations on the ankles caused by wearing tight socks.

Pluvigner (n.)

The minuscule hole in the side of a biro.

Plymouth (vb.)

To relate an amusing story to someone without remembering that it was they who told it to you in the first place.

Plympton (n.)

The knob on top of a war memorial.

Pocking (n.)

The pointless tapping of a cigarette before getting on with the business of smoking it.

Podebrady (n.)

The man in dirty overalls hired to wander whistling round the corridors of a large corporation to make it look as if the management's getting something done.

Pofadder (n.)

A snake that can't be bothered to bite you.

Poffley End (n.)

The green bit of a carrot.

Poges (pl.n.)

The lumps of dry powder that remain after cooking a packet of soup.

Polbathic (adj.)

Gifted with the ability to manipulate taps using only the feet.

Pollatomish (adj.)

Peevish, restless, inclined to pull the stuffing out of sofas.

Polloch (n.)

One of those tiny ribbed-plastic and aluminium foil tubs of milk served on trains enabling you to carry one safely back to your compartment where you can spill the contents all over your legs in comfort trying to get the bloody thing open.

Polperro (n.)

The ball, or muff, of soggy hair found clinging to bath overflow-holes.

Polyphant (n.)

The mythical beast – part bird, part snake, part jam stain

– which invariably wins children's painting competitions in the 5–7 age group.

Pontybodkin (n.)
The stance adopted by a seaside comedian which tells you that the punchline is imminent.

Poona (n.)
Satisfied grunting noise made when sitting back after a good meal.

Potarch (n.)
The eldest male in a soap opera family.

Pott Shrigley (n.)
Dried remains of a week-old casserole, eaten when extremely drunk at two a.m.

Prague (vb.)
To declaim loudly and pompously upon any subject about which the speaker has less knowledge than at least one other person at the table.

Preston Gubbals (n.)
Breasts of uneven weight.

Princes Risborough (n.)
The right of any member of the Royal Family to have people laugh at their jokes, however weedy.

Prungle (adj.)
Pretending to be proud to be single.

Pudsey (n.)
The curious-shaped flat wads of dough left on a kitchen table after someone has been cutting scones out of it.

Pulverbatch (n.)
The first paragraph on the blurb of a dust-jacket in which famous authors claim to have had a series of menial jobs in their youth.

Puning (ptcpl.vb.)

Boosting a man's ego by pretending to be unable to open a screwtop jar.

Pymble (n.)

Small metal object about the size of a thimble which lies on the ground. When you kick it you discover it is the top of something buried four feet deep.

Q

Quabbs (pl.n.)

The substances which emerge when you squeeze a blackhead.

QUABBS

Quall (vb.)

To speak with the voice of one who requires another to do something for them.

Quedgeley (n.)

A rabidly left-wing politician who can afford to be that way because he married a millionairess.

Quenby (n.)

A stubborn spot on a window which you spend twenty minutes trying to clean off before discovering it's on the other side of the glass.

Querrin (n.)

A person that no one has ever heard of who unaccountably manages to make a living writing prefaces.

Quoyness (n.)

The hatefulness of words like 'relionus' and 'easiphit'.

R

Radlett (n.)

The single hemisphere of dried pea which is invariably found in an otherwise spotlessly clean saucepan.

Ramsgate (n.)

All institutional buildings must, by law, contain at least twenty ramsgates. These are doors which open the opposite way to the one you expect.

Randers (pl.n.)

People who, for their own obscure reasons, try to sleep with people who have slept with members of the Royal Family.

Ranfurly (adj.)

Fashion of tying ties so that the long thin end dangles below the short fat end.

RANFURLY

Ravenna (n.)

Poetic term for the cleavage in a workman's bottom that peeks above the top of his trousers.

Rhymney (n.)

That part of a song lyric which you suddenly discover you've been mishearing for years.

Riber (n.)

The barely soiled sheet of toilet paper which signals the end of the bottom-wiping process.

Richmond (adj.)

Descriptive of the state that very respectable elderly ladies get into if they have a little too much sherry, which, as everyone knows, does not make you drunk.

Rickling (ptcpl.vb.)

Fiddling around inside a magazine to remove all the stapled-in special offer cards that make it impossible to read.

Rigolet (n.)

As much of an opera as most people can sit through.

Rimbey (n.)

The particularly impressive throw of a frisbee which causes it to be lost.

Ripon (vb.)

(Of literary critics) To include all the best jokes from the book in the review to make it look as if the critic thought of them.

Risplith (n.)

The burst of applause which greets the sound of a plate smashing in a canteen.

Rochester (n.)

One who is able to gain occupation of the armrests on both sides of their cinema or aircraft seat.

Roosebeck (n.)

Useful all-purpose emergency word. When a child asks 'Daddy, what's that bird/flower/funny thing that man's wearing?' you simply reply 'It's a roosebeck, darling.'

Royston (n.)

The man behind you in church who sings with terrific gusto almost three-quarters of a tone off the note.

Rudge (n.)

An unjust criticism of your ex-girlfriend's new boyfriend.

Rufforth (n.)

One who has the strength of character or loudness of voice to bring a lowthering (q.v.) session to an end.

S

Sadberge (n.)

A violent green shrub which is ground up, mixed with twigs and gelatine and served with clonmult (q.v.) and buldoo (q.v.) in a container referred to for no known reason as the 'relish tray'.

Saffron Walden (n.)

A particular kind of hideous casual jacket that nobody wears in real life, but which is much favoured by Ronnie Barker.

Salween (n.)

A faint taste of washing-up liquid in a cup of tea.

Samalaman (n.)

One who fills in the gaps in conversations by beaming genially at people and saying 'Well, well, well, here we all are then', a lot.

Satterthwaite (vb.)

To spray the person you are talking to with half-chewed breadcrumbs or small pieces of whitebait.

Saucillo (n.)

A joke told by someone who completely misjudges the temperament of the person to whom it is told.

Savernake (vb.)

To sew municipal crests on to an anorak in the belief that this makes the wearer appear cosmopolitan.

Scackleton (n.)

Horizontal avalanche of cassettes that slides across the interior of a car as it goes round a sharp corner.

Scamblesby (n.)

A small dog which resembles a throw-rug and appears to be dead.

SCAMBLESBY

Scethrog (n.)

One of those peculiar beards-without-moustaches worn by religious Belgians and American scientists which help them look like trolls.

Sconser (n.)

A person who looks around them when talking to you, to see if there's anyone more interesting about.

Scopwick (n.)

The flap of skin which is torn off your lip when trying to smoke an untipped cigarette.

Scorrier (n.)

A small hunting dog trained to snuffle amongst your private parts.

Scosthrop (vb.)

To make vague opening or cutting movements with the hands when wandering about looking for a tin opener, scissors, etc., in the hope that this will help in some way.

Scrabby (n.)

A curious-shaped duster given to you by your mother which on closer inspection turns out to be half an underpant.

Scrabster (n.)

One of those dogs which has it off on your leg during tea.

Scramoge (vb.)

To cut oneself whilst licking envelopes.

Scranton (n.)

A person who, after the declaration of the bodmin (q.v.), always says, '. . . But I only had the tomato soup.'

Scraptoft (n.)

The absurd flap of hair a vain and balding man grows long above one ear to comb it plastered over the top of his head to the other ear.

Screeb (vb.)

To make the noise of a nylon anorak rubbing against a pair of corduroy trousers.

Screggan (n.)

(Banking) The crossed-out bit caused by people putting the wrong year on their cheques all through January.

Scremby (n.)

The dehydrated felt-tip pen attached by a string to the 'Don't Forget' board in the kitchen which has never worked in living memory but which no one can be bothered to throw away.

Scridain (n.)

The tone that Norman Tebbit adopts with interviewers.

Scroggs (pl.n.)

The stout pubic hairs which protrude from your helping of moussaka in a cheap Greek restaurant.

Scronkey (n.)

Something that hits the window as a result of a violent sneeze.

Scugog (n.)

One whose mouth actually hangs open when watching

something mildly interesting on the other side of the street.

Scullet (n.)

The last teaspoon in the washing up.

Scurlage (n.)

A duck-web of snot caused by sneezing into your hand.

Seattle (vb.)

To make a noise like a train going along.

Shalunt (n.)

One who wears Trinidad and Tobago T-shirts on the beach in Bali to prove they didn't just win the holiday in a competition or anything.

Shanklin (n.)

The hoop of skin around a single slice of salami.

Sheepy Magna (n.)

One who emerges unexpectedly from the wrong bed-room in the morning.

Sheppey (n.)

Measure of distance (equal to approximately seven-eighths of a mile), defined as the closest distance at which sheep remain picturesque.

Shifnal (n.)

An awkward shuffling walk caused by two or more people in a hurry accidentally getting in the same segment of a revolving door.

Shimpling (ptcpl.vb.)

Lying about the state of your life in order to cheer up your parents.

Shirmers (pl.n.)

Tall young men who stand around smiling at weddings as if to suggest that they know the bride rather well.

Shoeburyness (n.)

The vague uncomfortable feeling you get when sitting on a seat which is still warm from somebody else's bottom.

Shottle (n.)

One of those tubes made of yellow plastic dustbins which builders use to get rubble off the top floor of a house.

Shrenk (n.)

A fold in a pair of stockings that aren't tight enough for a pair of thin legs.

Sicamous (adj.)

Perfectly willing to appear on the Terry Wogan show.

Sidcup (n.)

A hat made from tying knots in the corners of a hand-kerchief.

Sigglesthorne (n.)

Anything used in lieu of a toothpick.

Silesia (n.)

(Medical) The inability to remember, at the critical moment, which is the better side of the boat to be seasick off.

Silloth (n.)

Something that was sticky, and is now furry, found on the carpet under the sofa on the morning after a party.

Simprim (n.)

The little movement of false modesty by which a woman with a cavernous visible cleavage pulls her skirt down over her knees.

Sittingbourne (n.)

One of those conversations where both people are waiting for the other one to shut up so they can get on with their bit.

Skagway (n.)
Sudden outbreak of cones on a motorway.

Skannerup (n.)
A Swedish casserole made of elk-livers.

Skegness (n.)
Nose excreta of a malleable consistency.

Skellister (n.)
A very, very old solicitor.

Skellow (adj.)
Descriptive of the satisfaction experienced when looking at a really good drystone wall.

Skenfrith (n.)
The flakes of athlete's foot found inside socks.

Sketty (n.)
Apparently self-propelled little dance a beer glass performs in its own puddle.

Skibbereen (n.)
The noise made by a sunburned thigh leaving a plastic chair.

Skoonspruit (n.)
The tiny garden sprinkler thing your mouth sometimes does for no apparent reason.

Skrubburdnut (n.)
One who draws penises on posters of women in the Underground.

Skulamus (n.)
Someone who is obviously not doing what they went into the lavatory for.

Slabberts (pl.n.)
People who say 'Can I have some more juice?' when they mean gravy.

Slettnut (n.)

Something which goes round and round but won't come off.

Slipchitsy (n.)

Someone who takes the morning off work in order to sign on.

Slobozia (n.)

A chronic inability to pick up underpants.

Slogarie (n.)

Hillwalking dialect for the stretch of concealed rough moorland which lies between what you thought was the top of the hill and what actually is.

Sloinge (n.)

A post self-abuse tristesse.

Sloothby (adj.)

Conspicuously inconspicuous – as of a major celebrity entering a restaurant with a great display of being incognito.

Slubbery (n.)

The gooey drips of wax that dribble down the sides of a candle.

Sluggan (n.)

A lurid facial bruise which everybody politely omits to mention because it's obvious that you had a punch-up with your spouse last night – but which was actually caused by walking into a door. It is useless to volunteer the true explanation because nobody will believe it.

Slumbay (n.)

The cigarette end someone discovers in the mouthful of lager they have just swigged from a can at the end of a party.

Smarden (vb.)

To keep your mouth shut by smiling determinedly through your teeth.

Smardening is largely used by people trying to give the impression that they're enjoying a story they've heard at least six times before.

Smearisary (n.)
The part of a kitchen wall reserved for the schooltime daubings of small children.

Smisby (n.)
The correct name for a junior apprentice greengrocer whose main duty is to arrange the fruit so that the bad side is underneath.
From the name of a character not in Dickens.

Smyrna (n.)
The expression on the face of one whose joke has gone down rather well.

Sneem (n.)
Particular kind of frozen smile bestowed on a small child by a parent in mixed company when question, 'Mummy, what's this?' appears to require the answer, 'Er . . . it's a rubber johnny, darling.'

Snitter (n.)
One of the rather unfunny newspaper clippings pinned to an office wall, the humour of which is supposed to derive from the fact that the headline contains a name similar to that of one of the occupants of the office.

Snitterby (n.)
Someone who pins up snitters (q.v.).

Snitterfield (n.)
Office noticeboard on which snitters (q.v.), cards saying 'You don't have to be mad to work here, but if you are, it helps!!!' and smutty postcards from Ibiza get pinned up by snitterbies (q.v.).

Snoul (n.)
The third recurrence of a winter cold.

Snover (n.)

One who is reduced to drinking coffee from his egg-cups in order to put off the washing up just one more week.

Solent (adj.)

Descriptive of the state of serene self-knowledge reached through drink.

Soller (vb.)

To break something in two while testing if you glued it together properly.

Sompting (n.)

The practice of dribbling involuntarily into one's own pillow.

Sotterley (n.)

Uncovered bit between two shops with awnings, which you have to cross when it's raining.

Southwick (n.)

A left-handed wanker.

Spiddle (vb.)

To fritter away a perfectly good life pretending to develop film projects.

Spinwam (n.)

The toxic foam that clings to rocky foreshores.

Spittal of Glenshee (n.)

That which has to be cleaned off castle doors in the morning after a bagpipe-playing contest or vampire attack.

Spoffard (n.)

An MP whose contribution to politics is limited to saying 'Hear Hear'.

Spofforth (vb.)

To tidy up a room before the cleaning lady arrives.

Spokane (vb.)

To remove precious objects from a room before a party.

Spreakley (adj.)

Irritatingly cheerful in the morning.

Spruce Knob (n.)

A genital aftershave which is supposed to be catching on in America.

Spurger (n.)

One who in answer to the question 'How are you?' actually tells you.

Spuzzum (n.)

A wee-wee which resembles a lawn sprinkler, caused by a shred of tissue paper covering the exit hole of the penis.

Squibnocket (n.)

That part of a car, the unexpected need for the replacement of which causes garage bills to be four times larger than the estimate.

Stagno di Gumbi (n.)

(Italian) Pissed off with waiting for a bus to arrive, a waiter to bring the menu, or a genius to finish painting your ceiling.

Staplow (n.)

A telephone number that you now can't find anywhere because two years ago you swore you would never speak to the person again.

Stebbing (n.)

The erection you cannot conceal because you are not wearing a jacket.

Steenhuffel (n.)

One who is employed by a trade delegation or negotiating team to swell the numbers and make it look impressive when they walk out. There are currently 25,368 steen-huffels working at the UN in New York.

Stelling Minnis (n.)

A traditional street dance. This lovely old gigue can be seen at any time of the year in the streets of the City of London or the Courts of the Old Bailey. Wherever you see otherwise perfectly staid groups of bankers, barristers or ordinary members of the public moving along in a slightly syncopated way you may be sure that a stelling minnis is taking place. The phenomenon is caused by the fact that the dancers are trying not to step on the cracks in the pavement in case the bears get them.

Stibb (n.)

An unwelcome poke in the ribs by someone who hardly knows you.

'Mr Robert Maxwell stibbed Her Royal Highness repeatedly with his huby.' *The Times*.

Stibbard (n.)

The invisible brake pedal on the passenger's side of the car.

Stody (n.)

A small drink which someone nurses for hours so they can stay in the pub.

Stoke Poges (n.)

The tapping movements of an index finger on glass made by a person futilely attempting to communicate with either a tropical fish or a Post Office clerk.

Stowting (ptcpl.vb.)

Feeling a pregnant woman's tummy.

Strassgang (n.)

German word for the group of workers hired to lunch inside a string of motorway cones, or skagway (q.v.).

Strelley (n.)

Long strip of paper or tape which has got tangled round the wheel of something.

Strubby (adj.)

Attractively miniature.

Sturry (n.)

A token run. Pedestrians who have chosen to cross a road immediately in front of an approaching vehicle generally give a little wave and break into a sturry. This gives the impression of hurrying without having any practical effect on their speed whatsoever.

Stutton (n.)

Tiny melted plastic nodule which fails to help fasten a duvet cover.

Suckley Knowl (n.)

A plumber's assistant who never knows where the actual plumber is.

Surby (adj.)

Insolently polite, as of policemen who have stopped a motorist.

Sutton and Cheam (ns.)

Sutton and Cheam are the two kinds of dirt into which all dirt is divided. 'Sutton' is the dark sort that always gets on to light-coloured things, and 'cheam' the light-coloured sort that always clings on to dark items. Anyone who has ever found Marmite stains on a dress-shirt, or seagull goo on a dinner jacket a) knows all about sutton and cheam, and b) is going to some very curious dinner parties.

Swaffham Bulbeck (n.)

An entire picnic lunchtime spent fighting off wasps.

Swanage (pl.n.)

A series of diversionary tactics used when trying to cover up the existence of a glossop (q.v.) such as uttering a high-pitched laugh and pointing out of the window.

Swanibost (adj.)

Completely shagged out after a hard day having income tax explained to you.

Swefling (ptcpl.vb.)

Using a special attachment to Hoover a sofa.

Symond's Yat (n.)

The little spoonful inside the lid of a recently opened boiled egg.

T

Tabley Superior (n.)

The look directed at you in a theatre bar during the interval by people who've already got their drinks.

Tampa (n.)

The sound of a rubber eraser coming to rest after dropping off a desk in a very quiet room.

Tananarive (vb.)

To announce your entrance by falling over the dustbin in the drive.

Tanvats (pl.n.)

Disturbing things that the previous owners of your house have left in the cellar.

Tarabulus (n.)

The geometrical figure which describes the Ban the Bomb sign or a car steering wheel.

Taroom (vb.)

To make loud noises during the night to let the burglars know you are in.

Teigngrace (n.)

> The belief that a Devon cream tea is not going to make you feel sick after you've eaten it.

Tew (n.)

> Tuft of hair that grows between a man's eyebrows.

Tewel (n.)

> The little brass latch which fastens the front wall of a doll's house.

Throcking (ptcpl.vb.)

> The action of continually pushing down the lever on a pop-up toaster in the hope that you will thereby get it to understand that you want it to toast something.

Throckmorton (n.)

> The soul of a departed madman: one of those now known to inhabit the timing mechanisms of pop-up toasters.

Thrumster (n.)

> The irritating man next to you in a concert who thinks he's the conductor.

Thrupp (vb.)

> To hold a ruler on one end of a desk and make the other end go bbddbbddbbrrbrrrddrr.

Thurnby (n.)

> A rucked-up edge of carpet or linoleum which everyone says someone will trip over and break a leg unless it gets fixed. After a year or two someone trips over it and breaks a leg.

Tibshelf (n.)

> Criss-cross wooden construction hung on a wall in a teenage girl's bedroom which is covered with glass bambis and poodles, matching pigs and porcelain ponies in various postures.

Tidpit (n.)
The corner of a toenail from which satisfying little black spots may be sprung.

Tillicoultry (n.)
The man-to-man chumminess adopted by an employer as a prelude to telling an employee that he's going to have to let him go.

Timble (vb.)
(Of small nasty children) To fall over very gently, look around to see who's about, and then yell blue murder.

Tincleton (n.)
A man who amuses himself in your lavatory by pulling the chain in mid-pee and then seeing if he can finish before the flush does.

Tingewick (n.)
The first, sleepy morning stirrings of the penis.

Tingrith (n.)
The feeling of silver paper against your fillings.

Tockholes (pl.n.)
The tiny meaningless perforations which infest brogues.

Todber (n.)
One whose idea of a good time is to stand behind his front hedge and give surly nods to people he doesn't know.

Todding (ptcpl.vb.)
The business of talking amicably and aimlessly to the barman at the local.

Tolob (n.)
The crease or fold in an underblanket the removal of which involves getting out of bed and largely remaking it.

Tolstachaolais (phr.)

What the police in Leith require you to say in order to prove that you are not drunk.

Tomatin (n.)

The chemical from which tinned tomato soup is made.

Tonypandy (n.)

The voice used by presenters on children's television programmes.

Toodyay (n.)

Indonesian expression meaning 'sometime next month'.

Tooting Bec (n.)

A car behind which one draws up at the traffic lights and hoots at when the lights go green before realizing that the car is parked and there is no one inside.

Torlundy (n.)

Narrow but thickly grimed strip of floor between the fridge and the sink unit in the kitchen of a rented flat.

Toronto (n.)

Generic term for anything which comes out in a gush despite all your careful efforts to let it out gently, e.g. flour into a white sauce, tomato ketchup on to fried fish, sperm into a human being, etc.

Totteridge (n.)

The ridiculous two-inch hunch that people adopt when arriving late for the theatre in the vain hope that it will minimize either the embarrassment or the lack of visibility for the rest of the audience.

Trantlemore (vb.)

To make a noise like a train crossing a set of points.

Trewoofe (n.)

A very thick and heavy drift of snow balanced precariously on the edge of a door porch awaiting for what it judges to be the correct moment to fall.

From the ancient Greek legend, 'The Trewoofe of Damocles'.

Trispen (n.)

A form of intelligent grass. It grows a single, tough stalk and makes its home on lawns. When it sees the lawnmower coming it lies down and pops up again after it has gone by.

Trossachs (pl.n.)

The useless epaulettes on an expensive raincoat.

Trunch (n.)

Instinctive resentment of people younger than you.

Tuamgraney (n.)

A hideous wooden ornament that people hang over the mantelpiece to prove they've been to Africa.

Tukituki (n.)

A sexual liaison which is meant to be secret but which is in fact common knowledge.

Tullynessle (n.)

An honest attempt to track down a clitoris.

Tulsa (n.)

A slurp of beer which has accidentally gone down your shirt collar.

Tumby (n.)

The involuntary abdominal gurgling which fills the silence following someone else's intimate personal revelation.

TUAMGRANEY

Tweedsmuir (collective n.)

The name given to the extensive collection of hats kept in the downstairs lavatory which don't fit anyone in the family.

Twomileborris (n.)

A popular East European outdoor game in which the first person to reach the front of the meat queue wins, and the losers have to forfeit their bath plugs.

U

Udine (adj.)

Not susceptible to charm.

Ugglebarnby (n.)

The ponytail affected by a middle-aged balding man.

Ullapool (n.)

The spittle which builds up on the floor of the orchestra pit of the Royal Opera House.

Ullingswick (n.)

An over-developed epiglottis found in middle-aged coloraturas.

Ulting (ptcpl.vb.)

Clicking the jaw to unpop the ears.

Umberleigh (n.)

The awful moment which follows a dorchester (q.v.) when a speaker weighs up whether to repeat an amusing remark after nobody laughed the last time. To be on the horns of an umberleigh is to wonder whether people didn't hear the remark, or whether they did hear it and just didn't think it was funny, which was why somebody coughed.

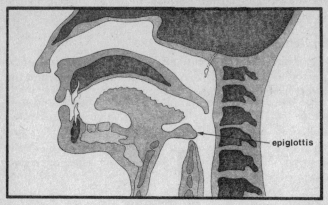

ULLINGSWICK

Upottery (n.)

That part of a kitchen cupboard which contains an unnecessarily large number of milk jugs.

Urchfont (n.)

Sudden stab of hypocrisy which goes through the mind when taking vows as a godparent.

Uttoxeter (n.)

A small but immensely complex mechanical device which is essentially the 'brain' of a modern coffee machine, and which enables the machine to take its own decisions.

V

Valletta (n.)

An ornate head-dress or loose garment worn by a person in the belief that it renders them invisibly native and not like tourists at all. People who don huge conical straw coolie hats with 'I luv Lagos' on them in Nigeria, or fat solicitors from Tonbridge on holiday in Malaya who insist on appearing in the hotel lobby wearing a sarong know what we are on about.

Vancouver (n.)

The technical name for one of those huge trucks with whirling brushes on the bottom used to clean streets.

Ventnor (n.)

One who, having been visited as a child by a mysterious gypsy lady, is gifted with the strange power of being able to operate the air-nozzles above aeroplane seats.

Vidlin (n.)

The moistly frayed end of a piece of cotton thread.

'It is easier for a rich man to enter the Kingdom of Heaven than it is for a vidlin to pass through the eye of a needle.'

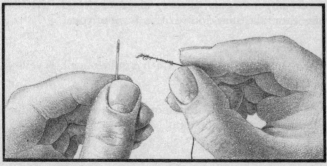

VIDLIN

Visby (n.)

The pointy, tent-like structure in the bedclothes with which a man indicates to his partner that he thinks it's high time she stopped fiddling around in the bathroom cupboard and came to bed.

Vollenhove (n.)

One who indicates from thirty yards across a crowded street that they have spotted you, wish to speak with you, and that you are required to remain rooted to the spot waiting for them.

Waccamaw (n.)

An exotic Brazilian bird which makes its home in the audiences of BBC Light Entertainment radio shows and screeches when it hears the word 'bottom'.

Warleggan (n.)

(Archaic) One who does not approve of araglins (q.v.).

Wartnaby (n.)

Something you only discover about somebody the first time they take their clothes off in front of you.

Wasp Green (adj.)

The paint in the catalogue which is quite obviously yellow.

Watendlath (n.)

The bit of wood a cabbie removes so as to open his sliding window and give you the full benefit of his opinions.

Wawne (n.)

A badly suppressed yawn.

Wedderlairs (pl.n)

The large patches of sweat on the back of a hot man's T-shirt.

WEDDERLAIRS

Wembley (n.)

The hideous moment of confirmation that the disaster presaged in the ely (q.v.) has actually struck.

Wendens Ambo (n.)

(Veterinary term) The operation to trace an object swallowed by a cow through all its seven stomachs. Hence, also, an expedition to discover where the exits are in the Barbican Centre.

West Wittering (ptcpl.vb.)

The uncontrollable twitching which breaks out when you're trying to get away from the most boring person at a party.

Wetwang (n.)

A moist penis.

Whaplode Drove (n.)

A homicidal golf stroke.

Whasset (n.)

A business card in your wallet belonging to someone whom you have no recollection of meeting.

Whissendine (n.)

A noise which occurs (often by night) in a strange house, which is too short and too irregular for you ever to be able to find out what it is and where it comes from.

Widdicombe (n.)

The sort of person who impersonate trimphones.

Wigan (n.)

If, when talking to someone you know has only one leg, you're trying to treat them perfectly casually and normally, but find to your horror that your conversation is liberally studded with references to (a) Long John Silver, (b) Hopalong Cassidy, (c) the Hokey Cokey, (d) 'putting your foot in it', (e) 'the last leg of the UEFA competition', you are said to have committed a wigan.

Wike (vb.)

To rip a piece of sticky plaster off your skin as fast as possible in the hope that it will (a) show how brave you are and (b) not hurt.

Willimantic (adj.)

Of a person whose heart is in the wrong place (i.e. between their legs).

Wimbledon (n.)

The last drop which, no matter how much you shake it, always goes down your trouser leg.

Winkley (n.)

A lost object which turns up immediately you've gone and bought a replacement for it.

Winster (n.)

One who is mistakenly under the impression that they are charming.

Winston-Salem (n.)

A person in a restaurant who suggests to their companions that they should split the cost of a meal equally, and then orders two packets of cigarettes on the bill.

Wivenhoe (n.)

The cry of alacrity with which a sprightly eighty-year-old breaks the ice on the lake when going for a swim on Christmas Eve.

Woking (ptcpl.vb.)

Standing in the kitchen wondering what you came in here for.

Wollondilly (n.)

A woman who can't get her lipstick on straight.

Worgret (n.)

A kind of poltergeist which specializes in stealing new copies of the A–Z from your car.

Worksop (n.)

A person who never actually gets round to doing anything because he spends all his time writing out lists headed 'Things To Do (Urgent)'.

Wormelow Tump (n.)

Any seventeen-year-old who doesn't know about anything at all in the world other than bicycle gears.

Wrabness (n.)

The feeling after having tried to dry oneself with a damp towel.

Writtle (vb.)

Of a steel ball, to settle into a hole.

Wroot (n.)

A short little berk who thinks that by pulling on his pipe and gazing shrewdly at you he will give the impression that he is infinitely wise and 6ft 2in.

Wubin (n.)

The metal foil container which Chinese meals come in.

Wyoming (ptcpl.vb.)

Moving in hurried desperation from one cubicle to another in a public lavatory trying to find one which has a lock on the door, a seat on the bowl and no brown streaks on the seat.

Y

Yalardy (n.)

An illness which you know you've got but which the thermometer refuses to acknowledge.

Yarmouth (vb.)

To shout at foreigners in the belief that the louder you speak, the better they'll understand you.

Yate (n.)

Dishearteningly white piece of bread which sits lumpily in a pop-up toaster during a protracted throcking (q.v.) session.

Yebra (n.)

A cross between a zebra and anything else which fancies zebras.

Yesnaby (n.)

A 'yes, maybe' which means 'no'.

YEBRA

Yetman (n.)

A yesman waiting to see who it would be most advantageous to agree with.

Yonder Bognie (n.)

The kind of restaurant advertised as 'just three minutes from this cinema' which clearly nobody ever goes to and, even if they had ever contemplated it, have certainly changed their minds since seeing the advert.

Yonkers (n.)

(Rare) The combined thrill of pain and shame when being caught in public plucking your nostril hairs and stuffing them into your side-pocket.

York (vb.)

To shift the position of the shoulder straps on a heavy bag or rucksack in a vain attempt to make it seem lighter.

Hence: to laugh falsely and heartily at an unfunny remark.

'Jasmine yorked politely, loathing him to the depths of her being.' – Virginia Woolf

Z

Zafrilla (n.)

A garment that even Lady Rothermere would not deign to wear.

Zagreb (n.)

A stranger who suddenly clutches an intimate part of your body and then pretends they did it to prevent themselves falling.

Zeal Monachorum (n.)

(Skiing term) To ski with 'zeal monachorum' is to descend the top three-quarters of the mountain in a quivering blue funk, but on arriving at the gentle bit just in front of the restaurant to whizz to a stop like a victorious slalom champion.

Zeerust (n.)

The particular kind of datedness which afflicts things that were originally designed to look futuristic.

ZIGONG

Zigong (n.)

Screeching skid made by cartoon character prior to turning round and running back in the opposite direction.

Zlatibor (n.)

(Hungarian) A prince of the blood royal temporarily forced to seek employment as a waiter.

Zod (n.)

An irritating lump which sticks out from the main body. Hence:
(1) A bit of cement which sits proud of the brickwork.
(2) A drip of paint on the windowpane.
(3) The knob of surplus butter on a corner of toast.
(4) Noel Edmonds' head.

Zumbo (n.)

One who pretends not to know that the exhaust has fallen off his car.

Index of Meanings

A

ABUSE
scissor: *Nogdam End*
self, post: *Sloinge*
self, sinister: *Southwick*

ACQUAINTANCES
remote: *Ardcrony*
who should be more remote:
Corfu

ACRONYMS, uselessness of: *Cafu*

ACTORS
dreadful, amateur: *Aberbeeg*
dreadful, fruity: *Hordle*
dreadful, lopsided: *Oundle*
dreadful, obese: *Pantperthog*
dreadful, Scottish, cravat-
wearing: *Glenduckie*
dreadful, Shakespearian:
Damnaglaur
dreadful, stained: *Multan*

ADAIR, RED: *Esher*

AFTERNOON
four o'clock in the: *Brymbo,
Farnham*
wasted in front of the television:
Gonnabarn

AIRPORTS
behaviour of luggage in: *Adlestrop*
cursed: *Aird of Sleat*

ALARMS
burglar: *Framlingham*
false: *Godalming*
silent: *Duleek*
untimely: *Lostwithiel*

ALBANIA, unpleasant beverages of:
Naas

ALGAE, trouser: *Huttoft*

AMERICANS
brain-dead: *Lackawanna*
strange, hairy: *Scethrog*

who aren't fooling anybody:
Ompton

AMOUNTS
contentious: *Bodmin*
footling: *Kibblesworth*
piddling: *Le Touquet*

ANATOMY
alarming discoveries about
someone's: *Wartnaby*
close proximity between bits of:
Moisie
confusion between bits of:
Willimantic
corrugations on bits of:
Plumgarths, Des Moines
horrible bits of: *Aigburth*
huge dangly strands of:
Ullingswick
hunts for bits of: *Tullynessle*
lovers who are keen on bits of
your: *Lublin*
odd connections between bits of:
Acklins
strangers who are keen on bits of
your: *Zagreb*
sweaty bits of: *Elsrickle, Pitsligo*
too frequently honoured parts of:
Dubbo
unwelcome bits of somebody
else's: *Stibb*
useless bits of: *Brecon, Clun*
wide open bits of: *Scugog*

ANIMALS
attempts to communicate with
Post Office clerks or: *Stoke Poges*
casual cross-breeding of: *Yebra*
disgusting bits of: *Gruids*
disinclination to be bothered to
identify: *Parrog, Roosebeck*
doo-doos of (china): *Barstibley*
doo-doos of (metaphorical):
Euphrates, Old Cassop

114

doo-doos of (real): *Dogdyke,
Joliette, Bromsgrove*
eviscerated, Swedish: *Skannerup*
fried: *Toronto*
haughty: *Pofadder*
mythical, or at least
unrecognizable: *Polyphant*
things that are like bits of:
Scurlage
with absurd numbers of
stomachs: *Wendens Ambo*

ANKLES
bits above your: *Bogue*
corrugated: *Plumgarths*

ANORAKS
cosmopolitan: *Savernake*
nylon: *Screeb*

ANSWERS
deflected: *Ainderby Steeple*
expected: *Nome*
required, embarrassing: *Sneem*
the phone, confusion caused
when someone: *Gammersgill*
the phone, suspicion caused
when someone: *Kurdistan*
unwelcome, interminable:
Spurger

ANTIQUES
telephone: *Aldclune*
useless, definitely fake: *Brumby*
useless, possibly fake: *Lydd*

ANTS, means of chasing: *Monks Toft*

APOLOGIES
loud, interminable: *Hickling*
recursive: *Greeley*
uttered while hopping: *Droitwich*

APPLAUSE
calculated to generate: *Firebag*
for injury: *Hoddlesdon*
ironic, in canteen: *Risplith*

ARCHDEACONS, protuberances on
the noses of: *Botolphs*

ARGUMENTS
after meals: *Bodmin*
after parties: *Heanton Punchardon*
badly planned: *Eakring*
before meals: *Lowther*
chilly consequences of: *Famagusta*
imperceptibly reversed: *Glenties*
manifestly blithering: *Inverinate*
uncharacteristically pertinent:
Gress

ARMHOLES
difficulties with: *Hessle*
excessive number of: *Jurby*

ARMRESTS, double helping of:
Rochester

ARMS
expanding: *Penge*
limp: *Oundle*
sweat under: *Pitsligo*

AROMAS
domestic, unwelcome: *Keele*
hireable, unwelcome: *Duluth*
rural, welcome: *Hull*
urban, unwelcome: *Chicago*
urban, welcome: *Lindisfarne*
zoological, romantic: *Dunbar*

ARTS
ancient, Eastern: *Kalami*
ancient: *Alltami*
domestic, sculptural: *Hepple*

ASHTRAYS
things used as: *Slumbay*
washing of: *Keele*

ASLEEP
bits of you that are: *Clun*
bits of you that aren't any more:
Tingewick
things collected while:
Ambatolampy
things heard while: *Balzan, Bonkle*

ASSISTANTS
exorcists': *Clenchwarton*
plumbers': *Suckley Knowl*
shop: *Hotagen*

ATTACHMENT
to a face: *Kirby*
to a Hoover: *Swefling*
to a nose: *Botolphs*
to a string: *Scremby*

ATTACKS
spasmodic: *Jawcraig*
vampire: *Spittal of Glenshee*

ATTEMPTS
kindly, misguided: *Kirby
Misperton*
lecherous, resolute: *Tullynessle*
lecherous, unsuccessful:
Farrancassidy
to see the film you've paid good
money to watch: *Ossining*

AWNINGS, gushing: *Sotterley*

INDEX of MEANINGS

B

BABIES
muckiness of: *Papple*
stickiness of: *Halcro*
second thoughts about the names
of: *Abert*

BACKS
of armchairs: *Hassop*
of cupboards: *Cong*
of people who are not your
friends: *Boothby Graffoe*
of T-shirts: *Wedderlairs*
of taxis: *Low Ardwello*
of throats: *Gulberwick*
things dropped down: *Burton
Coggles*

BACKSLAPPING: *Boothby Graffoe*
BADER, SIR DOUGLAS: *Ludlow*
BAFFLEMENT, nuptials marked by:
Cowcaddens

BAGS
carrier, growing: *Dungeness*
elderly, deaf: *Nanhoron*
fearsome, hideous: *Baughurst*
mulch kept in the bottom of: *Glud*
paper, maternal: *Marlow*
slippery, translucent: *Flimby*
solitary, Scottish: *Glentaggart*

BAKERS
least appealing products of:
Brymbo
people who show off to:
Bradworthy

BALDNESS
graceless reactions to: *Ugglebarnby*
useless attempts to conceal:
Scraptoft

BALLADS, raucous old: *Banteer*
BALLS
dangerous number of: *Belding*
soggy, hairy: *Polperro*
steel, rattling: *Writtle*

BANDS, rubber: *Monks Toft*
BANKS
rising young managers of:
Hobarris
things that confuse: *Albuquerque,
Screggan*
Welsh: *Pen tre-tafarn-y-fedw*

BARBICAN CENTRE, the: *Wendens
Ambo*

BARMEN
aimless: *Todding*
apparently blind: *Epping*
surly: *Goole*

BARRISTERS
dancing: *Stelling Minnis*
greasy: *Glazeley*

BARS
complete berks in: *Louth*
sandwich: *Darenth*
theatre: *Tabley Superior*
wet: *Listowel, Goole*

BASINS
things found in: *Misool,
Hathersage*
things washed in: *Paradip*

BASTARDS
bloody rude: *Fovant*
in technical sense: *Gastard*
inconsiderate, stupid, filthy:
Dogdyke
lazy: *Abinger, Ozark*
mad and/or lazy: *Boseman*
scatty: *Abligo*
six year old: *Little Urswick*
smooth, beery: *Louth*
smooth, young: *Shirmers*
smug, Masonic: *Grimsby*
vile, vain, rich: *Shalunt*

BATHROOMS
attempts to lure people out of:
Visby
nocturnal attempts to find:
Islesteps

BATHS
bubbly noises in: *Budle*
prunelike objects in: *Dewlish*
round, rubbery objects in: *Dillytop*
soggy things in: *Polperro*
turbulent convection in: *Harlosh*

BATS
hairy, harmless old: *Lossiemouth*
incompetent, well-meaning old:
Jurby
stout, wooden: *Pelutho*
vampire: *Spittal of Glenshee*

BATTLEAXES, sharp, on castle
wall: *Pabbay*

BDDBBRRDDBDDRR, things that
go: *Thrupp*

BEATING: *Aboyne*
BED
areas to be avoided in: *Hobbs Cross*

116

banana-shaped objects on:
Baumber
comforting preparations for:
Lambarene
dreadful mistakes in: *Hagnaby*
tent-shaped objects in: *Visby*
things found in: *Ballycumber*
things that bounce on: *Abwong,
Dunster*
things that don't work in: *Stutton*
things that go wrong in: *Brecon*
things that jump out of: *Duleek*
thrashing around in: *Oswestry*
unwelcome lumps in: *Tolob*

BEDROOMS
chilly winds in: *Famagusta*
embarrassing things in hotel:
Bedfont
emerging from wrong: *Sheepy
Magna*
guests in spare: *Dunster*
views into other people's: *Beaulieu
Hill*
young girls': *Tibshelf*

BEHAVIOUR
facetious, misguided: *Dockery*
lip: *Gallipoli*
naughty: *Sheepy Magna*
nurdlike: *Scugog*
perverse, sticky: *Ardslignish*

BEHIND
cleavage in: *Ravenna*
dragging one leg: *Oundle*
droplets on: *Elsrickle*
leaving one's hat: *Hidcote Bartram*

BELGIANS, hairy, religious:
Scethrog

BELIEFS
creamy, mistaken: *Teignmouth*
fatuous, entertained abroad:
Valletta, Yarmouth
mistaken, humorous: *Dockery*

BERKS
check-jacketed, beery: *Louth*
deliberately forgetful: *Abligo*
in restaurants: *Ardentinny*
irritatingly conversational:
Dalmilling
lazy: *Nybster*
short, pipe-smoking: *Wroot*
unwanted: *Nubbock*
who can't tell jokes without

making a complete hash of
it: *Jofane*
BICYCLEGEARS: *Wormelow Tump*
BILLS
anomalous: *Bodmin*
heart-stopping: *Squibnocket*
sneakily inflated: *Winston-Salem*
BIRD
Brazilian, easily amused:
Waccamaw
possible congruence with type of:
Parrog
sort of half-: *Polyphant*
unidentifiable: *Roosebeck*
BIROS
holes in: *Pluvigner*
leaky: *Pen tre-tafarn-y-fedw*
three-coloured: *Ospringe*
tied together, six: *Ipplepen*
BISCUITS
digestive, religious: *Corstorphine*
fresh, or so they claim: *Dorridge*
BITES
snakes which can't be bothered to
administer: *Pofadder*
spots which could be: *Bauple*
BLISS
conjugal, absence of at dinner:
Balemartine, Inigonish
conjugal, absence of in bed:
Famagusta
conjugal, absence of in car:
Heanton Punchardon
conjugal, conducted on cheap
floor-matting: *Bures*
conjugal, first steps back towards:
Manitoba
conjugal, invitation to: *Visby*
conjugal, possible threats to:
Kurdistan
conjugal, recurrent threats to:
Mavis Enderby
of a really good widdle: *Gilling*
BLOBS
bloody-minded: *Glossop*
dried: *Klosters*
stubborn: *Quenby*
BLOWOUTS, oral: *Berkhamsted*
BLUEFUNK: *Zeal Monachorum*
BLUEMURDER: *Timble*
BOARDS, don't forget: *Scremby*
BOOKREVIEWS: *Ripon*

BOOKS
 codswallop in: *Pulverbatch*
 fat, expensive: *Great Tosson*
 futile attempts to read: *Dalmilling*
 incomprehensible paragraphs in:
  Fritham
 lavatorial: *Great Wakering*
 of matches, not worth stealing:
  Fremantle
 triumphantly finished: *Beppu*
 you haven't finished: *Ballycumber*
 you haven't read at all: *Bathel*
BOOKSHELVES: *Ahenny*
BORES
 low tolerance of: *Lolland*
 pompous, any age: *Ardcrony*
 principal habitat of: *Burslem*
 things induced by: *Wawne*
 worst, at a party: *West Wittering*
BOTTLE PARTIES: *Naas, Aasleagh*
BOTTLES
 blue: *Bursledon*
 gin: *Le Touquet*
 ketchup: *Cromarty*
 whisky: *Brumby*
BOTTOM
 chill wind that afflicts: *Famagusta*
 cleavage in workman's: *Ravenna*
 exposed: *Grinstead*
 huge whirling brushes on:
  Vancouver
 interesting patterns on own:
  Kettering
 lip: *Gallipoli*
 newly cleaned: *Riber*
 of drawers, things found in:
  Pimlico
 of shoes: *Luppitt*
 reaction of Brazilian bird to
  mention of: *Waccamaw*
 rivulets between cheeks of:
  Elsrickle
 warmth of someone else's:
  Shoeburyness
BOXES
 of chocolates: *Bolsover*
 in garages: *Kentucky*
BOYS
 high-pitched: *Caarnduncan*
 new: *Percyhorner*
 with stupid names: *Cheb*
BRAIN
 inoperative: *Duntish*

 of coffee machine: *Uttoxeter*
BRAS
 impossible: *Farrancassidy*
 inadequate: *Lusby*
BREAD
 airborne crumbs of: *Satterthwaite*
 hundred slices of: *Darenth*
 single slice of: *Yate*
 wildlife in: *Mankinholes*
BREAK
 a leg: *Thurnby*
 into something that clearly isn't a
  run: *Sturry*
 something you've just glued
  together: *Soller*
 the ice: *Wivenhoe*
 up, are they going to?:
  Badachonacher
BREASTS
 attempted access to: *Farrancassidy*
 clumsy business with: *Meadle*
 lopsided: *Preston Gubbals*
 only semi-contained: *Lusby*
BREATH
 condensation of: *Brithdir*
 extruded through noses: *Burbage*
BREEZES, in armpit: *Kimmeridge*
BRISTLES: *Aith*
BRONSON, CHARLES: *Duncraggon*
BRUISES
 honourably acquired: *Dubbo*
 virulent, accidental: *Sluggan*
 yellowing, inexplicable: *Ampus*
BUBBLES
 behind wallpaper: *Lupridge*
 congealed, cheesy: *Eriboll*
 flatulent: *Budle*
 slurped, milky: *Pitlochry*
BUFFERS
 boring, old: *Ainderby Quernhow*
 insane, sprightly old: *Wivenhoe*
 loathsome, merry old: *Boothby
  Graffoe*
 pompous old: *Ainderby Steeple*
BUILDERS
 bottoms of: *Ravenna*
 murderous: *Hodnet*
 rubble-removing techniques of:
  Shottle
BULBS
 light: *Fring*
 that die when you look at them:
  Lutton Gowts

INDEX *of* MEANINGS

CLOTS, mad, patronizing:
Largoward

CODGERS
boring, famous, old: *Boothby Graffoe*
huge, wobbling, wheezing, old: *Kingston Bagpuise*
stuffy, medieval, old: *Warleggan*

COFFEE
not quite enough: *Pidney*
noxious substances in: *Cadomin*

COFFEE-MACHINES, intelligent:
Uttoxeter

COINS
domestic, vital: *Nupend*
foreign, assorted: *Boolteens*
foreign, unwanted: *Bindle*

COLD
ears, hearty feelings induced by:
Luffness
swimming pool, nearly brave enough to dive into: *Parbold*
third recurrence of winter: *Snoul*
taps, hot and, deft handling of:
Alltami

COLLECTIONS
awful record: *Hextable*
charity: *Ardelve*
eccentric: *Aldclune*
somnambulent: *Ambatolampy*

COLOUR
biros, three-: *Ospringe*
depressingly wrong: *Gretna Green*
multi-purpose, municipal: *Frating Green*
of paints in catalogues: *Wasp Green*
red, virulent: *Buldoo*
supplements, hideous containers for: *Mapledurham*

COMBS, clogged: *Haselbury Plucknett*

COMMISSIONAIRES
boring: *Clabby*
swinish: *Margate*

COMPLAINTS
tiresome: *Mogumber*
very tiresome: *Ainderby Quernhow*

COMPONENTS
small, meaningless: *Pimlico*
vital, missing: *Exeter*

CONCEPTS
hitherto unnamed: *Liff*

that people won't grasp perfectly simple: *Osbaston*

CONFETTI
overabundance of: *Pathstruie*
royal: *Didcot*

CONTAINERS
Chinese meal: *Wubin*
ludicrously misnamed: *Sadberge*

CONTEST, bagpipe: *Spittal of Glenshee*

CONTRIBUTIONS
negligible: *Spoffard*
very public, probably negligible:
Ardelve

CONVERSATIONS
desired: *Affcot*
gaps in: *Samalaman*
interminable: *Ditherington*
polite, interminable: *Clabby*
polite, pointless: *Sittingbourne*
shifting: *Glenties*
thuggish: *Jawf*
wasted: *Harpenden*

CORDS
electrical, that get pulled back:
Lynwilg
swimming-trunk, that get lost:
Lubcroy

CORNWALL, mood on contemplating trip to: *Offleyhoo*

CORRIDORS
cowardly behaviour in:
Corriecravie
etiquette in: *Corriearklet*
hideous mistimings in:
Corriemoillie
making pig's ear of walking down: *Corriemuchloch*
pretending to be Richard Briers in: *Corriedoo, Corrievorrie*

COSIES
spare toilet-roll: *Ossett*
tee: *Kitmurvy*

COTTAGES
retirement: *Duncraggon*
weekend: *Hull*

COUGHS
gurgling: *Brisbane*
that don't seem to have any effect: *Gulberwick*
throaty: *Dorchester*

COUPLES
arguing loudly: *Heanton Punchardon*
arguing most of the time: *Badachonacher*
arguing silently: *Famagusta*
no longer arguing: *Manitoba*
pretending not to be arguing: *Nyarling*

COWS
journeys through: *Wendens Ambo*
things left in fields by: *Munderfield*

CRAFTWORK: *Dalrymple*

CRAVAT, worn by Scottish actors: *Glenduckie*

CREAM
anti-wrinkle: *Melton Constable*
ice-: *Badgebup*

CREEPS
boring: *West Wittering*
embarrassing realization about identity of: *East Wittering*

CRIMES, ancient: *Burlingjobb*

CRISES, humorous exploitation of: *Gribun*

CROSS
a road too slowly: *Sturry*
a road, not about to: *Boseman*
activities indulged in while: *Burleston*
things that make you: *Draffan, Hickling*
with zebra: *Yebra*

CROSSINGS
pedestrian: *Boseman*
train: *Trantlemore*

CROTCHES, TROUSER: *Botley, Piddletrenthide*

CROUCHES, upward: *Hucknall*

CRY
end of a: *Mointy*
ill-equipped to: *Hankate*
reason to: *Babworth*

CUBICLES
inaccessible: *Milwaukee*
horribly soiled: *Wyoming*

CUPBOARDS
bathroom, attempts to lure people out of: *Visby*
jugs in: *Upottery*
kites in: *Kanturk*
saucepans in: *Cong*
skeletons in: *Glemanuilt*

CURSES, Scottish: *Aird of Sleat*
CUSHIONS, roadside: *Edgbaston*

D

DAMOCLES, the Trewoofe of: *Trewoofe*

DANCES
in street: *Droitwich, Stelling Minnis*
of beer glasses: *Sketty*
people who won't ask people for: *Peening Quarter*
Polynesian, that the Queen has to sit through: *Grutness*

DEARIES
lovable, mad old: *Bradworthy*
soporific rabbity old: *Clabby*

DECISIONS
minor, agonizing: *Deventer*
right, agonizing: *Abalemma*
wrong, agonizing: *Huna*

DECORATIONS, CHRISTMAS: *Clovis, Chenies*

DENTISTS
activities of unemployed: *Beccles*
results of going to: *Gallipoli, Gipping*

DEPARTURES
inability to make: *Foffarty*
of madmen: *Throckmorton*
welcome, of others: *Nubbock*

DEPOSITS
crystalline: *Libenge, Klosters*
pink, sticky: *Glud*
sludgy: *Cromarty*
small, black, satisfying: *Tidpit*

DESKS
useful things that fall off: *Tampa*
useless things that stay on: *Kilvaxter*

DESPERATION
polite: *Iping*
frankly rushed: *Wyoming*

DETERMINATION
bloody-minded: *Oswestry*
politely restrained: *Kent, Calicut, Smarden*

DEVICES
agricultural: *Jarrow*
humorous: *Barstibley*
immensely complex: *Uttoxeter*

INDEX *of* MEANINGS

E

EARS
fears concerning: *Loberia*
inner: *Nanhoron, Ulting*
outer: *Luffness*
EARTHQUAKES, humorous:
Drumsna
EDICTS, ancient: *Farduckmanton*
EGGS
boiled: *Symond's Yat*
coffee drunk from receptacle
designed for: *Snover*
scrambled: *Cloates Point*
EIGHTY-YEAR-OLDS, bounding,
refrigerated: *Wivenhoe*
ELBOWS
damp: *Listowel*
sexually active, sore: *Bures*
territorially intrusive: *Rochester*
EMOTIONS
angry, unmusical: *Burleston*
cheerful: *Spreakley, Abwong*
infinitely sad: *Glasgow*
susceptibility of: *Cahors*
triste: *Sloinge*
ENDS
damp, cigarette: *Slumbay*
long, thin, dangling: *Ranfurly*
of desks, uses of: *Thrupp*
of parties: *Aasleagh*
of recalcitrant pieces of cotton:
Vidlin
of toothbrushes: *Pibsbury*
ENGINEERS, telephone,
inexplicable marriages to: *Lydiard Tregoze*
ENTRIES
in diaries: *Epsom*
in drive: *Tananarive*
into Mecca: *Multan*
into the Kingdom of Heaven:
Vidlin
ENVELOPES
dangerous: *Scramoge*
deceitful: *Hugglescote*
empty: *Cannock Chase*
ENVIRONMENTS
dark, moist: *Huttoft*
urban, excremental: *Bromsgrove*
EPAULETTES, useless: *Trossachs*
EPIGLOTTIS, giant, waggling:
Ullingswick

ERASERS, rubber: *Tampa*
ESKIMO, sore thumbs of an:
Anantnag
EVENINGS
Friday, noisy: *Framlingham*
tense: *Heanton Punchardon*
wasted: *Lowther*
EVENTS, lack of: *Chimkent*
EX-GIRLFRIEND
new boyfriend of: *Rudge*
wife's resentment of: *Mavis Enderby*
EXCRETA, airborne: *Burlingjobb*
EXCUSES
feeble: *Dorridge*
impromptu, but still feeble:
Hastings
incredible, unnecessary: *Falster*
indignant: *Hoff*
ludicrous: *Brisbane*
transparent: *Bilbster*
EXORCISM: *Clenchwarton*
EXPERIENCES
hitherto unnamed: *Liff*
horrific: *Maaruig*
lurching: *Bedfont*
melancholy: *Glasgow*
panicky: *Ditherington*
satisfying: *Skellow*
terrific: *Nempnett Thrubwell*
EXPERTS, humiliating the: *Aboyne*
EXPRESS, THE SUNDAY, people
who actually read the: *Molesby*
EXPRESSIONS
facial, agonized: *Minchinhampton*
peculiar: *Banff*
pissed: *Blithbury*
raging: *Damnaglaur*
sly: *Golant*
vaguely attentive: *Hove*
EYEBROWS
things that grow between: *Tew*
useless employment of: *Epping*

F

FACES
grubby: *Badgebup*
guilty: *Peru, Hastings*
silly: *Leeming, Banff*
warm and salty: *Moisie*

INDEX *of* MEANINGS

FAMILY
    arguments, odd behaviour
    during: *Gress*
    fictional, head of: *Potarch*
    hats that don't belong to the:
    Tweedsmuir
    Royal, head of the, being stoic in
    Indonesia: *Grutness*
    Royal, joke-telling privileges of
    the: *Princes Risborough*
    Royal, member of foreign, on
    uppers: *Zlatibor*
    Royal, sleeping with members of
    the: *Randers*
    Royal, understandable fears
    suffered by members of the:
    Loberia
    seaside-visiting: *Molesby*

FARTS – *see under noises* (if you must)

FAT
    books: *Great Tosson*
    chance of actually winning
    £10,000: *Hugglescote*
    ends of ties: *Ranfurly*
    people: *Humber*
    solicitors: *Valletta*

FEARS
    anatomical: *Loberia*
    vegetable: *Peoria*

FEELINGS
    in unexpected parts of body:
    Acklins
    of fillings: *Tingrith*
    of something or other, profound:
    Hambledon
    queasy, bottom-orientated:
    Shoeburyness
    queasy: *Guernsey*
    sentimental: *Glasgow*
    sofa-threatening: *Pollatomish*
    tired, cold, thirsty: *Luffenham*
    uneasy: *Dungeness, Frating Green*

FEET
    damp, pink, wrinkled: *Dewlish*
    elephantine, umbrellas for the
    use of: *Clackmannan*
    painful: *Nipishish*
    tingling sensations in: *Gilling*
    with highly developed tap skills:
    Polbathic

FENCING: *Pabbay*

FESTOONMENT: *Chipping Ongar*

FIFTEEN YEARS
    at the same desk: *Brough Sowerby*
    younger than you, people who
    are: *Glasgow*

FILMS
    pornographic: *Papworth Everard*
    rewritten ends of famous:
    Epworth
    that won't get made: *Spiddle*

FINGERS
    definitely not green: *Lutton Gowts*
    insertion of, into: *Cannock Chase*
    lecherous: *Farrancassidy,
    Tullynessle*
    not within reach of: *Nad*
    things that cling to: *Mummelgum,
    Ardslignish, Dipple*

FISH
    tropical, stupid: *Stoke Poges*
    overabundance of heads of:
    Chimbote

FLAMES
    almost-completely-forgotten old:
    Mavis Enderby
    people you wish were old: *Lydiard
    Tregoze*
    reminders of old: *Mavesyn
    Ridware*

FLAPS
    clothy, roomy: *Moffat*
    hairy, sparse: *Scraptoft*
    leathery: *Luppitt*
    muddy: *Fladderbister*

FLATS
    grimy: *Torlundy*
    too far from the shops: *Nantwich*

FLEMING, SIR ALEXANDER:
    Eriboll

FLIES: *Harbottle*

FLOORMATTING, indelicate uses
    of: *Bures*

FLUFF
    mysterious: *Knaptoft*
    navel: *Lowestoft*
    yellow: *Memphis*

FOLDS
    bothersome: *Tolob*
    fleshy: *Lusby*
    silky: *Shrenk*

FOOD
    ethnic, inedible: *Chimbote*
    inappropriate: *Kowloon*
    misnamed: *Slabberts*

railway, inedible: *Amlwch*
sculptable: *Hepple*
shortly going to be inedible:
Cloates Point
unequal divisions of: *Finuge*
very little actual, packets
containing: *Dorridge*
FOOTBALLERS, pansy: *Hoddlesdon*
FOREIGNERS
impersonation of: *Aberbeeg*
probably deaf or stupid: *Yarmouth*
FOREPLAY
at a distance: *Visby*
clumsy: *Meadle*
reconciliatory: *Manitoba*
vocal: *Low Ardwello*
FOWL-FEEDING: *Farduckmanton*
FREEMASONS
banned practices of: *Enumclaw*
ritual pieces of gristle, use of by:
Grimsby
FRIDGES
concealed matter in: *Goosnargh*
concealed matter rediscovered
three weeks later in: *High Offley*
damp things in: *Nantwich*
strips of floor next to: *Torlundy*
teeming with life: *Guernsey*
FRIENDS
or so they would like to think:
Peterculter, Ardcrony, Boothby
Graffoe
unmarried: *Canudos*
FROWNING, important: *Frolesworth*
FRUIT
in the manner of: *Hordle*
stupid overabundance of:
Limassol
theft of a single piece of: *Market*
Deeping
FURNITURE
air-expelling: *Essendine*
bamboo, disintegration of:
Blitterlees
execrable: *Mapledurham*
lavatorial: *Ossett*

G

GABLE, CLARK: *Epworth*
GAMES
ball: *Hoddlesdon, Pelutho*

board: *Bishop's Caundle,*
Hoggeston
indoor: *Aboyne*
outdoor, Eastern
European: *Twomileborris*
GARDENING
equipment, piece of, mysterious:
Haxby
hopelessness of: *Crail*
trousers used for: *Broats*
GARDENS
alarming sheds in: *Low*
Eggborough
embarrassing talks in: *Ambleside*
GARMENTS
discussions about making:
Gussage
ethnic, inapposite: *Nokomis*
exotic, pretentious: *Shalunt*
fatuous, foreign: *Valletta*
funny one that man's wearing:
Roosebeck
gaberdine, ankle-length:
Flodigarry
loose, hateful, well-intentioned:
Anjozorobe
naff material for making: *Joplin*
peculiar, frightful: *Neen Sollars*
preposterous: *Zafrilla*
removed with dispiriting results:
Wartnaby
semi-inverted: *Hessle*
that don't fool anybody: *Ompton*
too loose: *Shrenk*
woollen, knee-length: *Jurby*
GAZES, shrewd, berkish: *Wroot*
GENITALS
moist: *Wetwang*
moved about by owner: *Grobister*
moved about by selves: *Tingewick*
solitary recreational uses of:
Southwick, Sloinge
washed politely: *Paradip*
well-groomed: *Spruce Knob*
GESTURES, ambiguous but bloody
rude: *Fovant*
GIBBERISH
argumentative: *Inverinate*
nocturnal: *Burslem*
telephonic: *Harpenden,*
Gammersgill
that issues from cars: *Addis Ababa*
GIN, price of: *Le Touquet*

GIRLFRIEND
  long forgotten except by wife:
  Mavis Enderby
  resentment concerning: *Rudge*

GIRLS
  coiffured: *Aubusson*
  naff epistolary habits of: *Ocilla*
  pot-brandishing: *Kittybrewster*
  teenage, in bedroom: *Tibshelf*

GIZMOS
  plastic, metal, Bakelite: *Pimlico*
  small, clever: *Uttoxeter*
  tasteless: *Barstibley*

GLANCES
  humorous, at blobs: *Swanage*
  meaningful: *Balemartine*

GLASS
  pointless scraping at: *Quenby*
  pointless tapping on: *Stoke Poges*

GLOBULES, yellow, gummy,
  unpleasant: *Mugeary*

GO
  bbddbbddbbrrbrrrrddrr, things
  that: *Thrupp*
  off, alarms that don't: *Duleek*
  people who finally: *Nubbock*
  people who just won't: *Clunes*
  to the lavatory, urgent need to:
  Great Wakering
  trying unsuccessfully to: *Foffarty*

GOATS
  jocular tedious old: *Barstibley*
  noisy tuneless old: *Royston*

GOLFING, overpaid twats who go:
  Kitmurvy

GOLFSTROKES, homicidal:
  Whaplode Drove

GOO
  seagull: *Sutton and Cheam*
  waxy: *Slubbery*

GOODBYES, premature: *Hidcote
  Bartram*

GOSSIP
  bubbling with: *Malaybalay*
  judicious applications of:
  Marytavy
  subject of immense amount of:
  Tukituki

GOURMETS, slithery: *Berry Pomeroy*

GRASS
  absence of: *Abruzzo*
  intelligent forms of: *Trispen*

GRAVEL
  infuriating: *Crail*
  walking barefoot on: *Nipishish*

GRIDS, cattle: *Humber*

GROCERS, green: *Halifax, Smisby*

GROUND
  things buried four feet in the:
  Pymble
  toxic waste: *Caarnduncan*
  up: *Sadberge*
  worn away: *Abruzzo*

GROUPS
  infuriatingly indecisive: *Lowther*
  of five that should be four:
  Lampeter
  peer: *Caarnduncan*
  that exclude you: *Margaretting Tye*

GUARDS, railway: *Galashiels*

GUILT
  powerful: *Glemanuilt*
  surprised: *Peru*

GUMBOOTS
  cold: *Luffness*
  wet: *Burwash*

GUNGE
  crystalline: *Libenge*
  damp, gummy: *Deal*
  green, shrubby: *Sadberge*
  pinkish: *Glud*
  unwholesome: *Mummelgum*

GURGLING
  involuntary, abdominal: *Tumby*
  perfectly reasonable explanation
  for: *Brisbane*   ·
  through straws: *Pitlochry*

GUSTO, terrific, tuneless: *Royston*

GUTTERS, dog's business clogging
  up the: *Dogdyke*

H

HAIR
  armpit, ruffled: *Kimmeridge*
  facial, bizarre: *Scethrog*
  few last strands of: *Scraptoft*
  greasy, legal: *Glazeley*
  paint damage caused by: *Garrow*
  plucking of nostril: *Yonkers*
  pubic, in moussaka: *Scroggs*
  sprigs of, for chasing ants: *Monks
  Toft*
  tufty interocular bits of: *Tew*

unaccompanied: *Albacete*
unbecoming styles of: *Aubusson,
Ugglebarnby, Papigochic*
HANDLEBAR MOUSTACHES,
female: *Lossiemouth*
HANDS
clammy: *Meath*
psychologically helpful
movements of the: *Scosthrop*
rubbed: *Ardentinny*
slimy: *Scurlage*
HANGOVERS, incapacitating:
Duntish
HANKIES
lack of: *Hankate*
peered into: *Massachusetts*
worn on head: *Sidcup*
HAT BEHIND, leaving one's:
Hidcote Bartram
HATRED, violent, by spouse: *Mavis
Enderby*
HATS
furry, absurd: *Glinsk*
gigantic, conical: *Valletta*
large, ill-fitting collection of:
Tweedsmuir
naff: *Sidcup*
HEADS
alarming numbers of fish:
Chimbote
black: *Quabbs*
of state, poorly: *Patkai Bum*
HEALTHY, hopeless attempts to
become: *Berkhamsted, Elgin,
Kingston Bagpuise*
HEDGE, things to do behind one's
front: *Todber*
HERRING FISHERMEN: *Flodigarry*
HISTORY, lost in the mists of:
Hutlerburn
HOLES
bath overflow: *Polperro*
in biros: *Pluvigner*
in toothbrushes: *Pibsbury*
things which get stuck over:
Spuzzum
things which settle into: *Writtle*
things which sit on: *Dillytop*
HOLIDAYS
impressively unencumbered:
Nuncargate
naïve behaviour on: *Valletta*
not won in competitions: *Shalunt*

people met on: *Corfu*
things brought home from:
Glassel, Jubones, Anjozorobe
HOME
at BBC Radio studios, birds that
make their: *Waccamaw*
people who'd rather go: *Lowther*
stuff that turns up in your:
Mavesyn Ridware
things that don't look good at:
Jubones
things that happen on the way:
Heanton Punchardon
things that might be at:
Mankinholes
time to go: *Inigonish*
HOOKS
jammy: *Halcro*
picture, things for banging in:
Nogdam End
HOOVER
putting away a: *Lynwilg*
sofas: *Swefling*
under feet: *Hucknall*
HOPEFULNESS
misplaced, of being amusing:
Gaffney
naïve, regarding lunch: *Jeffers*
naïve, regarding tea: *Teigngrace*
of finding idiot: *Kibblesworth*
of getting better invitation: *Darvel*
HORNS
large, uncomfortable: *Humby*
long, ceremonial: *Hunsingore*
moderate-sized, but
unconcealable: *Huby*
small, Scandinavian: *Oswaldtwistle*
HORROR
conversational: *Wigan*
inexpressible: *Maaruig*
HORSES
china, rude: *Barstibley*
understandably irate: *Belding*
HOSTESSES, air: *Ewelme*
HOTELS
clothes ill-advisedly worn in:
Valletta
incredibly dull things in: Lamlash
mock-Tudor: *Melcombe Regis*
shambolic, clanking: *Bonkle*
HOUSES
dolls': *Tewel*
Opera, spittle in Royal: *Ullapool*

INDEX *of* MEANINGS

rented: *Delaware*
romantic doo-doos in reptile:
Dunbar
rubble removals from: *Shottle*
strange, dark: *Islesteps*
strange, noisy: *Whissendine*
things in the cellar of: *Tanvats*
White, amnesiacs in: *Esterhazy*
HUNCHES, foolish, in the theatre:
Totteridge
HUTLERS, clumsy: *Hutlerburn*
HYMNS
pitched at random: *Royston*
pitched too high or low: *Detchant*

theatre bars in the: *Tabley Superior*
INTO EACH OTHER
bumping: *Droitwich*
things that go: *Toronto*
INVITATIONS
obligatory: *Oughterby*
waited for: *Darvel*
ITEMS
nasal, airborne: *Scronkey*
prunelike, waterlogged: *Dewlish*
sticky, clammy: *Belper*
sticky, furry: *Silloth*
thin, circular, meaty: *Shanklin*

I

ICE, octogenarians under the:
Wivenhoe
IDEA
having a better: *Ferfer*
not having the faintest: *Epsom,
Osbaston*
very much his own: *Brough
Sowerby*
IDENTITY CARDS, left at home:
Margate
IDIOTS
roaring, pretentious: *Haugham*
ludicrous, deluded: *Kibblesworth*
IMPLEMENTS
curious, horticultural: *Haxby*
useless: *Ipplepen*
wooden, silly: *Ibstock*
INCOME TAX, impossibility of
understanding: *Swanibost*
INCONTINENCE, reptilian: *Dunbar*
INFANTS, small, naked, comical:
Barstibley
INFORMATIVE, disinclined to be:
Clixby
INKLINGS, tiny, stomach-curdling:
Ely
INTERESTING
how: *Nome*
mildly: *Scugog*
temporarily: *Glassel*
than you, someone more: *Sconser*
than your newspaper, more:
Corfe
INTERVAL
eight-month: *Peterculter*

J

JACKETS
dust: *Pulverbatch*
hairy, stained: *Bradford*
hideous casual: *Saffron Walden*
loud check: *Louth*
not quite long enough: *Stebbing*
things found in: *Nupend*
JAM
canteen, semi-delicious
ingredients of: *Masberry*
jars, coverings for: *Jid*
not worth stealing: *Fremantle*
used for fastening clothes: *Halcro*
JOGGING, suicide by means of:
Kingston Bagpuise
JOHNNIES, rubber: *Sneem, Phillack*
JOKES
decreasingly funny: *Gignog*
early warnings of ends of:
Pontybodkin
length of: *Gildersome*
medieval, practical: *Araglin*
mild for vicars: *Bude*
practical, spectacular: *Banteer*
technically inept: *Jofane*
told to wrong audience: *Saucillo*
well-received: *Smyrna*
JUDGES, things they have to put up
with: *Dockery, Glazeley*

K

KEYS
car, endless inability to find:
Dalfibble

129

L

INDEX *of* MEANINGS

LOOKS
frosty: *Gartness*
lecherous: *Frosses*
superior, at shoes: *Dubuque*
superior, in theatre: *Tabley Superior*
warning: *Balemartine*
wistful, unexplained: *Foping*

LOST
in any one of a number of places: *Kelling*
in the grass: *Rimbey*
in the mists of history: *Hutlerburn*
in the photocopier: *Dufton*
objects than turn up: *Winkley*
perpetually: *Dalfibble*
quickly becoming: *Brindle*

LOUDNESS
of apologies: *Hickling*
of declaimed opinions: *Prague*
of gurgling: *Pitlochry*
of jacket: *Louth*
of nocturnal noises: *Taroom, Bonkle*
of voice: *Rufforth, Yarmouth, Haugham, Lulworth*

LOUNGES, cocktail: *Melcombe Regis*

LOVE, unrequited: *Lydiard Tregoze*

LUGGAGE
economical with: *Nuncargate*
ill-behaved: *Adlestrop*

LUMPS
agricultural, aromatic: *Jarrow*
awkward, in trousers: *Stebbing*
cardboard, useful: *Ludlow*
disgusting, attached to face: *Kirby*
dull, in suitcase: *Glassel*
edible, steaming, irremovable: *Glossop*
gristly, acrid: *Grimsby*
gummy, shapeless: *Papcastle*
powdery, floating: *Poges*
small, awkward, dangerous: *Fraddam*
small, nasal: *Peebles*
tiny, in swimming trunks: *Lubcroy*
unwelcome, nocturnal, in front: *Humby*
unwelcome, nocturnal, underneath: *Tolob*
unwelcome, urban, all over: *Burlingjobb*

urban, overhead and underfoot: *Bromsgrove*
useless, that stick out: *Zod, Huby*

M

MAD, you don't have to be, etc: *Snitterfield*

MADMEN, departed, in toasters: *Throckmorton*

MAKE UP
kiss and: *Manitoba*
lopsided: *Wollondilly*

MANHOLES, open, amusing: *Frimley*

MANOEUVRES, awkward, leaping: *Hobbs Cross*

MAPS, road: *Kalami*

MARGARINE: *Darenth*

MARKETS, super: *Duggleby, Flimby, Motspur, Boscastle*

MATS, small, sopping: *Listowel*

MATTER, gaseous: *Eriboll*

MATTRESSES
banana-shaped: *Baumber*
enormous, muscular: *Harbledown*

MAYBE, meaning no: *Yesnaby*

MEALS
arguments about where to have: *Lowther*
arguments at the end of: *Bodmin*
hopelessly over-optimistic: *Jeffers*
light, nutritious, for busy playwrights: *Cresbard*
noises after: *Poona*
things they come in: *Wubin*
to avoid: *Skannerup*

MEANINGLESS
components, small: *Pimlico*
holes in brogues: *Tockholes*
letters to editor: *Dalderby*
noises, distant: *Amersham*
smiles, shiny: *Ewelme*

MEASURE OF LUMINOSITY: *Blean*

MEASURES OF DISTANCE
carparks: *Nad*
sheep: *Sheppey*
trousers: *Malibu*
tubes: *Frant*

MEASURES OF TIME
art galleries: *Frolesworth*

fishlike: *Gipping*
flabby: *Humber*
futile, at Post Offices: *Stoke Poges*
futile, at waiters: *Epping*
futile, in own house: *Kelling*
vague, manual, searching:
Scosthrop
waggling, artistic: *Llanelli*
MUMBLES, deliberate: *Inverkeithing*
MURMANSK, things that shouldn't
be in: *Glentaggart*
MUSH, dehydrated: *Pott Shrigley*
MUSIC
rendered weepy by old: *Cahors*
simple, played badly: *Dinsdale*

N

'N': *Nacton*
NAMES
being cute with: *Ocilla, Cheb*
cheating with: *Aalst*
execrable: *Drebley*
forgetting of: *Golant, Inverkeithing*
loves that dare not speak their:
Lyminster
sudden reconsidering of: *Abert*
NAP
conditions in which you should
try to have a: *Duntish, Hynish,
Cranleigh*
limbs having a: *Clun*
things brushed against the: *Nith*
NEAPOLITAN, tubs, fists shoved
into: *Blean*
NEEDLES
conversations that are largely
concerned with: *Gussage*
things that won't go through the
eyes of: *Vidlin*
NEW YORK
cluelessness in: *Lackawanna*
employment opportunities in:
Steenhuffel
NEWS, astounding: *Jawcraig*
NEWSPAPER
cuttings, comical: *Snitter*
fascination of someone else's:
Corfe
opinions gleaned from: *Macroy*
proprietors, monstrous:
Bickerstaffe

racks, bewildering fascination
with: *Condover*
NIGHT
dazedness during: *Lampung*
noises during: *Balzan,
Whissendine, Bonkle, Boinka*
things purloined during:
Ambatolampy
NIPPLES, high profile: *Budby*
NITWITS, great steaming: *Duggleby*
NO, expressed as yes: *Yesnaby*
NODS
surly, from behind hedge: *Todber*
thoughtful, vacant: *Dinder*
NODULES
plastic, melted: *Stutton*
rubber: *Pimperne*
NOISES
bodily, benign: *Bepton*
bubbling and inopportune:
Tumby
burbling and nocturnal: *Bonkle*
discreet but unwelcome: *Affcot*
distant and meaningless:
Amersham
grunting and considerate:
Horton-cum-Studley
gurgling and milky: *Pitlochry*
gushing and cooing: *Oshkosh*
humming and grinding: *Burleston*
humming and groaning:
Milwaukee
loud and clattering: *Clackmannan*
loud and deafening: *Balzan*
loud and embarrassing: *Berepper*
loud and informative: *Taroom*
loud and rattling: *Hoggeston*
loud and revolving: *Cairo*
minuscule, worrying: *Fring*
mumbling, uninterested: *Nazeing*
nocturnal, interminable:
Framlingham
nocturnal, intermittent:
Whissendine
painful and squeaky: *Skibbereen*
post-prandial: *Poona*
quiet and rubbery: *Tampa*
resounding from clifftops:
Craboon
screeching, Celtic: *Lochranza*
screeching, infantile:
Caarnduncan
squeaky, nylonish: *Screeb*

INDEX *of* MEANINGS

tatatting and satisfying: *Ibstock*
ticketatacketaticketting: *Seattle*
ticketatacktackatuckaticketting:
Trantlemore
triumphant and slappy: *Beppu*
trumpeting, hippopotamoid:
Brompton
warm and underwater: *Budle*
whiffling, in lifts: *Burbage*
whirring and chuntering: *Ipswich*

NOSES
adornments to: *Botolphs*
bleeding: *Burton Coggles*
erstwhile contents of: *Longniddry*
fascinating items in: *Massachusetts*
ill-equipped to deal with runny:
Hankate
noises made with: *Burbage*
things which are ejected from:
Scurlage
things which come down from:
Des Moines
things which stretch a long way
from: *Coilantogle*
tools for stuffing into:
Botusfleming

NOZZLES, aircraft, strange powers
over: *Ventnor*

NUMBERS
lost: *Staplow*
wrong, for any given purpose:
Pleven
wrong, of potatoes: *Peoria*
wrong, or so he claims: *Kurdistan*

NURDS
conferences for unwanted,
Absecon
excited: *Hugglescote*
incredible little: *Corfu*
piddling, in your lavatory:
Tincleton
preeping: *Widdicombe*
tittering, white-collar: *Snitterby*

O

OBJECTS
banana-shaped: *Baumber*
bloody-minded: *Ardslignish*
clammy, inedible: *Amlwch*
contented stares at: *Dallow,
Skellow*

creatively misapplied: *Botswana*
dangerously misleading: *Pymble*
deformed: *Duddo*
elephantine: *Clackmannan*
fantastically dull: *Lamlash*
flimsy, intriguing: *Corfu*
frilly: *Ossett*
heavy, with toes on: *Clun*
hidden, pointed: *Gilgit*
hideous, shelfbound: *Delaware*
hitherto unnamed: *Liff*
horrible, roomy: *Mapledurham*
innocent, repeatedly hit: *Ashdod*
Kenyan: *Jubones*
long-handled: *Botusfleming*
lost, found again: *Winkley*
massive, wooden, airborne: *Camer*
plastic, pretentious: *Brumby*
sticky, jam-infested: *Halcro*
sticky, permanent: *Dipple*
sticky, wooden: *Cotterstock*
strange, culinary: *Cong*
that don't fool anyone: *Zeerust*
tiny, disgusting: *Chipping Ongar*
tiny, pointless: *Didcot*
twelve, baffling: *Cowcaddens*
unappealing, lonely: *Brymbo*
wet, cold, enormous: *Trewoofe*
with bumps on: *Bolsover*
with holes in, artistic: *Bromsgrove,
Dalrymple*

OFFICERS, retired, army, raving:
Pant-y-Wacco

OFFICES
comical cuttings on walls of:
Snitter
fat chance of getting anything to
work properly in: *Podebrady*
lost pieces of paper in: *Dufton*
managers who hide in their:
Harmanger
people who decorate: *Clovis,
Snitterby*
resentful people in: *Brough
Sowerby*
scapegoats in: *Bickerstaffe*

OFFICIALS
people who become: *Benburb*
who make your life a misery:
Margate

OLDS
bounding, refrigerated, eighty-
year-: *Wivenhoe*

134

cringe-making, fourteen-year-: *Cheb*
on heat, sixteen-year-: *Frosses*
sweating, forty-year-: *Kingston Bagpuise*
ON, trying it: *Brabant*
OOZE, yellow: *Clonmult*
OPINIONS
confident, wrong: *Macroy*
hard to tolerate: *Chaling*
that taxi-drivers wish to share with you: *Watendlath, Crieff*
unasked-for, reverend: *Dean Funes*
ORCHESTRA PITS, spittle in: *Ullapool*
ORCHESTRAS
conducted from the audience: *Thrumster*
which spit a lot: *Ullapool*
ORGASM, MULTIPLE: *Papworth Everard*
ORNAMENTS, misapplied: *Bishop's Caundle*
wooden: *Tuamgraney*
OVERALLS, inky: *Hibbing*

P

PAGE
last, of book: *Beppu*
last, of document, left in photocopier: *Dufton*
single, blithering: *Clackavoid*
PAIN AND SHAME: *Yonkers*
PAINS, sudden: *Acle*
PAINT, smudges, expensive: *Dalrymple*
PAINTBRUSHES, cheap: *Aith*
PAINT-STIRRERS: *Cotterstock*
PANGS, terrible: *Lydiard Tregoze*
PANIC
in airport: *Hever*
in corridor: *Ditherington*
in lavatory: *Great Wakering*
PAPER
barely soiled toilet: *Riber*
silver, against teeth: *Tingrith*
tangled, spinning: *Strelley*
under lid: *Jid*
PARENTS
attempts to mislead: *Shimpling*

embarrassed: *Sneem*
god: *Urchfont*
parties given by: *Frosses*
PARTICLES, nasal: *Massachusetts*
PARTIES
adventurous behaviour at: *Hallspill*
crud under sofas after: *Silloth*
deposits acquired at curious dinner: *Sutton and Cheam*
dreadful guests at: *Nubbock, Oughterby*
frosty glances at dinner: *Inigonish*
heated recriminations after: *Heanton Punchardon*
irritatingly successful people at: *Draffan, Offord Darcy*
people to avoid at: *East Wittering, West Wittering*
political: *Firebag*
steamy, teenage: *Frosses*
things drunk in desperation at end of: *Aasleagh*
things found in lager cans at the end of: *Slumbay*
things found in wine glasses after: *Picklenash*
things removed from rooms before: *Spokane*
welcome departures from: *Nubbock*
women's conversational exclusiveness at: *Flums*
PARTS, private, had by dog for lunch: *Scorrier*
PATCHES
wet, under bottom: *Hobbs Cross*
wet, underarm: *Pitsligo*
PAVING STONES: *Affpuddle*
PEBBLES, wet, shiny: *Glassel*
PEDANTS: *Ainderby Quernhow*
PEE
foot-tingling sensations caused by: *Gilling*
inability to do with audience present: *Kettleness*
PELLETS, unmentionable: *Peebles*
PENCIL SHARPENINGS, giant: *Blitterlees*
PENISES
embarrassingly visible: *Stebbing*
embarrassingly visible, useless: *Huby*

INDEX *of* MEANINGS

for naming things, no known: *Sadberge*

for sleeping with people, obscure: *Randers*

for spray in your mouth, unknown: *Skoonspruit*

for staring at something, no particular: *Dallow*

REASSURANCE
much needed: *Godalming*
spurious: *Old Cassop*

RECEPTION
chilly: *Saucillo*
not very good: *Gweek*

RELATIONSHIPS
unresolved: *Badachonacher*
wish to sort out other people's: *Canudos*

RELEVANT
only slightly: *Juwain*
surprisingly: *Gress*

RELISH TRAYS: *Clonmult, Sadberge, Buldoo*

RELUCTANCE
feigned, easily overcome: *Climpy*
feigned, very easily overcome: *Alcoy*

REMARKS
calculated, crowd-pleasing: *Firebag*
own, rather amusing, unheard: *Dorchester, Umberleigh*
stoicism in the face of wounding: *Calicut*

REMOVALS
non-furniture: *Dipple, Grimsby, Rickling, Spokane, Tolob, Watendlath, Botusfleming, Crail*
piano: *Nundle*

REQUESTS, whining, unwelcome: *Quall*

RESTAURANTS
embarrassing manual behaviour in: *Ardentinny*
embarrassing vocal behaviour in: *Haugham*
perverse behaviour in: *Kowloon*

REVELATIONS, personal, with stomach-rumble: *Tumby*

RICHARD III: *Oundle*

RIGHTS
ancient, pebbly: *Pevensey*
ancient, with midgets: *Forsinain*

telling lefts from: *Memus, Noak Hoak*

RIPPING, of skin: *Wike*

ROADS, signposting of: *Botcherby*

ROCK, small pieces of, apparently limitless quantities of: *Crail*

ROLLS, sausage, stuff you wouldn't even find in: *Gruids*

ROUND
but don't come off, things that go: *Slettnut*
but shouldn't, things that go: *Strelley*
things that don't go: *Adrigole, Motspur*
things that go: *Hextable*

ROWING, accidents while: *Anantnag*

RUBBERS
noises made by: *Tampa*
places for keeping: *Phillack*
you didn't want to be asked about: *Sneem*

RUBBISH, vital, in dustcart: *Nottage*

RUCKSACKS: *York*

RUGS, horseshoe-shaped, fluffy: *Luton*

RULERS, noises made by: *Thrupp*

RUNS, token: *Sturry*

RYVITA, consistency of: *Naples*

S

SACHETS, impenetrable: *Naugatuck*

SACKING: *Tillicoultry*

SAFE PLACES: *Fiunary*

SALAMI: *Shanklin*

SANDWICHES
bacon: *Beccles*
in London: *Darenth*
on trains: *Amlwch*

SARONG, appearing in lobby wearing a: *Valletta*

SAUCEPANS
almost but not quite spotless: *Radlett*
chocolate-filled: *Abinger*

SAUNTERS, carefree: *Frimley*

SAUSAGES
in rolls: *Gruids*
stuff to smear on: *Patney*
twisted: *Kerry*

SCABS, amorous: *Bures*

SIDEBURNS, extensive, scrofulous:
Galashiels
SIGNPOSTS, pathetic attempt at
proper: *Botcherby*
SIGNS, to be taken seriously: *Belding*
SILENCES, ghastly: *Lulworth*
SINGERS
awful: *Royston*
carol, hiding from: *Fulking*
wailing: *Lochranza*
SINGLE
and proud of it, or so they claim:
Prungle
desire to see people stop being:
Canudos
hair: *Albacete*
men who are too groovy to dance:
Peening Quarter
SIX TIMES BEFORE, stories heard:
Smarden
SIXTEEN
stone men on last legs: *Kingston
Bagpuise*
-year-olds on heat: *Frosses*
SKIING: *Zeal Monachorum*
SKILLS
bath-filling: *Alltami*
cowardly: *Corriecravie*
loaf-naming: *Bradworthy*
revolting: *Oystermouth*
useless as it turns out: *Aboyne*
SKIN
flaps of: *Scopwick*
twists of: *Kerry*
expanses of: *Bogue*
SLEEP
larcenous behaviour during:
Ambatolampy
muck in eyes after: *Mugeary*
people with whom you're not
sure if you want to: *Libode*
things which might help you get
to: *Burslem*
things which prevent you getting
to: *Burleston, Framlingham*
things which interrupt your:
Lostwithiel, Dunster
things which shouldn't have gone
to: *Clun*
SLIMMING, feeble dishonest shot
at: *Berkhamsted*
SLOBS
complete: *Snover*

lazy: *Abinger*
SLUDGE
brittle: *Cromarty*
moist: *Eads*
SMELLS, horrible: *Keele*
SMILES
frozen, horrified: *Sneem*
grim, determined: *Smarden*
shiny, meaningless: *Ewelme*
SMOKING, excuses for: *Brisbane*
SMUTTY POSTCARDS: *Snitterfield*
SNACKS, nasty: *Nantwich*
SNEEZING
failure to: *Amersham*
horribly violent success at:
Scronkey
SNIPPETS, hairy: *Hathersage*
SNOW, wedges of lurking: *Trewoofe*
SOAP OPERA, Australian:
Clackavoid
SOCKS
contents of: *Senfrith*
things that appear above: *Bogue*
SOFA
restlessly plucked at: *Pollatomish*
things spotted from: *Chenies*
SOLICITORS
excessively elderly: *Skellister*
fat from Tonbridge: *Valletta*
SONG
misheard lyric of: *Rhymney*
Scottish folk: *Lochranza*
that makes you want to cry:
Cahors
SOPPING, shopping: *Sotterley*
SOUP
exotic, made from moats: *Bealings*
packet: *Poges*
splattered: *Papple*
tomato: *Scranton, Tomatin*
SPACE AND TIMELESSNESS:
Hambledon
SPASMS, massive facial: *Jawcraig*
SPEAKER
deliberately ovation-inducing:
Firebag
guest, absolute drivel concerning:
Euphrates
SPEECH
affected: *Pitroddie*
fatuous introduction to: *Euphrates*
parts of, crucial, obscured:
Dorchester

INDEX *of* MEANINGS

SPERM
 career-oriented: *Hobarris*
 copious quantities of: *Toronto*
 marooned, damp: *Hobbs Cross*
 marooned, dry: *Bedfont*
SPIT: *Gallipoli*
SPOONFUL
 eggy: *Symond's Yat*
 not quite a: *Pidney*
SPOTS
 bites which could be: *Bauple*
 to which you have to remain
 rooted: *Vollenhove*
SPRIGS, dangling, colourful:
 Chenies
SQUEEZING
 cosmetic: *Quabbs*
 religious: *Clenchwarton*
SQUIGGLES, financial: *Albuquerque*
STAINS
 inky: *Hibbing*
 Marmite: *Sutton and Cheam*
 trousers, own fault: *Piddletrenthide*
 trousers, not own fault: *Botley*
STAIRCASES, winding: *Harbledown*
STAIRS
 disappearing: *High Limerigg*
 falling down the: *Blean*
STANDING ABOUT: *Lowther*
STANDING AND WONDERING:
 Woking
STANDING, ways of: *Ahenny*
STARES
 harsh, meaningful: *Kurdistan*
 mellow, meaningless: *Dallow*
STATE
 disease of deposed heads of:
 Patkai Bum
 hungover: *Duntish*
 of barrister's hair: *Glazeley*
 of dress: *Grinstead*
 of mind: *Hynish, Pant-y-Wacco*
 of respectable ladies: *Richmond*
STEPS, small, irrevocable: *Glenties*
STEW, ghastly items found in:
 Grimsby
STEWART, ANDY: *Maaruig*
STICK
 out, things that: *Zod, Stebbing,
 Huby, Humby, Loberia*
 to the point: *Gress*
 to your skin, things that: *Wike*

together, things that shouldn't
 but do: *Dipple*
together, things that won't: *Soller,
 Badachonacher*
up, things that: *Visby, Pymble*
STICKS
 swiping with: *Hewish*
 walking: *Clackmannan*
STOMACHS
 expeditions through seven:
 Wendens Ambo
 lurching sensations in: *Bedfont*
STORIES
 endless, repetitive, celebrity:
 Boothby Graffoe
 humorous, heard before:
 Plymouth
 humorous, interminable:
 Gildersome
STRANGE POWERS OVER
 AIRCRAFT NOZZLES: *Ventnor*
STRANGER, than a zebra: *Yebra*
STRANGERS
 perfect, bewildering messages
 from: *Berriwillock*
 perfect, patronizing remarks
 made by: *Maynooth*
 perfect, who grab your naughty
 bits: *Zagreb*
STREAKS, brown: *Wyoming*
STREETS
 cleaning of: *Vancouver*
 epiglottises spotted on: *Scugog*
 exasperating encounters on:
 Vollenhove
STRIPS, grimy: *Torlundy*
STUBBLE
 in basin: *Hathersage*
 in sandwiches: *Munderfield*
STUMPS, tree: *Baldock*
SUBJECT
 declaimed ignorantly upon:
 Prague
 of property prices: *Munster*
 someone to unwelcome
 attentions: *Boothby Graffoe,
 Peterculter, Corfu*
SUBSTANCES
 brown, squashy: *Skegness*
 green, synthetic: *Halifax*
 grey, gummy: *Deal*
 ochre, indelicate: *Quabbs*
 yellow, dried: *Henstridge*

141

yellow, squelchy: *Mugeary*
white, flaky: *Skenfrith*
various colours, gushing: *Toronto*
SUNBATHING: *Kimmeridge,
Kettering*
SURPRISES
hair-induced: *Albacete*
unpleasant, at public school:
Percyhorner
SUSPICIONS
horrible: *Mankinholes*
of infidelity: *Kurdistan*
SWATTING: *Bursledon*
SWEAT
panther, erotic properties of:
Dunbar
patches of, enticingly displayed:
Pitsligo
patches of, large: *Wedderlairs*
small, moving beads of: *Elsrickle*
SWIGS, nasty surprises in: *Slumbay*
SWITCHES, useless: *Ockle*

T

TABLES
antique, priceless, ruined: *Glossop*
dressing, cluttered with garbage:
Boolteens, Lamlash
highly polished antique rosewood
dining: *Glossop*
inexpertly laid: *Fentonadle*
leapt on to: *Pabbay*
not laying: *Nanhoron*
shy behaviour near: *Namber*
things left on kitchen: *Pudsey*
things stuck under wobbly:
Ludlow
TACTICS
diversionary: *Swanage*
thwarted: *Aboyne*
TALKING, unlikelihood of
stopping: *Hove*
TANNOY, half heard: *Hever*
TAPS
foot-operated: *Polbathic*
pointless: *Pocking*
push, trouser-dousing: *Esher*
TARPAULINS: *Flodigarry*
TAXI-DRIVERS: *Fovant*
TAXIS
driven by idiots: *Lackawanna*

hypocrisy resorted to in: *Crieff*
opinions offered in: *Watendlath*
seductive remarks in: *Low
Ardwello*
smell of: *Duluth*
TEASPOON, the ultimate: *Scullet*
TEETH
feelings in: *Tingrith*
food stores between: *Glutt Lodge*
improvised things used to clean
between: *Sigglesthorne*
results of cleaning: *Misool*
things that might have been
caused by: *Bauple*
unwelcome views of: *Scugog*
TEETH, smiling determinedly
through: *Smarden*
TELEPHONE DIRECTORIES,
collectors of antique: *Aldclune*
TELEPHONES
embarrassing memory loss when
using: *Gammersgill*
inability to get off: *Harpenden*
numbers, misplaced: *Staplow*
suspicious number of wrong
numbers when answering:
Kurdistan
uselessness of: *Ipswich*
TELEVISION
afternoons wasted in front of:
Gonnabarn
celebrity, fat: *Melbury Bubb*
commercials, chuckles at the end
of: *Lybster*
interviewers, tone of voice
afflicted on: *Scridain*
newsreaders, determined not to
be embarrassed: *Hosmer*
presenters, tone of voice of:
Tonypandy
series based on books: *Bathel*
willing to be on: *Sicamous*
THEATRE, practices in: *Hickling,
Totteridge, Tabley Superior*
THIMBLES
conversations that probably touch
upon the subject of: *Gussage*
things that aren't: *Pymble*
THINGS
small, complex: *Uttoxeter*
small, pleasant: *Strubby*
small, worrying: *Exeter*
spray, for ironing: *Perranzabuloe*

INDEX *of* MEANINGS

to do: *Worksop*
various: *Sutton and Cheam*

TIES
  inelegantly knotted: *Ranfurly*
  innate cussedness of: *Clingman's Dome*

TIGHTS, misuse of: *Grinstead*

TINGLES
  apprehensive: *Ely*
  delightful: *Gilling*

TINS
  attempts to find things to open: *Scosthrop*
  biscuit: *Lindisfarne*
  of emulsion, stubborn: *Botswana*
  of soup: *Tomatin*
  pyramids of: *Boscastle*

TIPS, felt: *Scremby*

TOASTERS
  spirits that inhabit: *Throckmorton*
  uselessness of: *Yate, Burnt Yates*
  work, attempts to make: *Throcking*

TOBLERONES, consequences of triangular shape of: *Gubblecote*

TOENAILS, contents of: *Tidpit*

TOES, slime on: *Deal*

TOILETRIES
  misapplied: *Wollondilly*
  mixed: *Glud*
  rather naughty: *Spruce Knob*

TONGS, silver, for poking Freemasons: *Grimsby*

TONGUE
  things touched with: *Lingle, Moisie*
  unwelcome glimpses of: *Scugog*

TORCHES, dim: *Blean*

TOWELS, damp: *Wrabness*

TOXIC
  foreshores: *Spinwam*
  soup: *Tomatin*
  waste ground: *Caarnduncan*

TRACTORS, dung-spreading: *Jarrow*

TRAIN
  conversations on: *Jawf*
  departed without one: *Dunboyne*
  impersonation of: *Trantlemore, Seattle*
  inedible things on: *Amlwch*
  non-arrival of: *Amersham*
  Royal: *Didcot*

tickets: *Nantucket*

TREES
  Nigerian: *Masberry*
  stumps of: *Baldock*

TRIMPHONES, impersonation of: *Widdicombe*

TRIPPING OVER CARPET: *Thurnby*

TROLLEYS, rogue: *Motspur*

TROUSERS
  elderly: *Broats*
  inflatable: *Huby*
  roguish: *Minchinhampton*
  soaking: *Esher*
  stained: *Botley, Piddletrenthide*
  too long: *Malibu*
  wooden: *Goosecruives*
  wrong pair of: *Duggleby*

TROUTS, fierce old: *Baughurst*

TRUCKS, street-cleaning: *Vancouver*

TRUNKS, swimming: *Lubcroy*

TRUTH, palpable: *Hoff*

TUBES
  in London: *Amersham, Chicago, Frant*
  in meat: *Aigburth*
  in spring: *Pitsligo*

TUBS, impenetrable: *Polloch*

TUMMIES
  nasty feelings in pits of: *Ely*
  pregnant: *Stowting*
  sounds that emanate from: *Tumby*

TURDS
  (dog) comely, well-proportioned: *Joliette*
  (dog) small, but still nasty: *Bromsgrove*
  thick as your wrist: *Laxobigging*

TURN-UPS, fertile: *Huttoft*

TWATS, annoying: *Thrumster*

TWEEZERS, difficulty with: *Hadweenzic*

TWERPS, bicycle-oriented: *Wormelow Tump*

TWITCHING, uncontrollable: *West Wittering*

U

UMBRELLA STANDS: *Clackmannan*

143

INDEX *of* MEANINGS

UMBRELLAS
  absent when needed: *Sotterley,*
  Plenmeller
  in drinks, stupid little: *Limassol*
  things that aren't: *Dunolly*
UNDERBLANKETS, lumpy: *Tolob*
UNDERCLOTHES, bestrewn:
  Adlestrop
UNDERPANT, half an: *Scrabby*
UNDERPANTS
  floorbound: *Slobozia*
  incomplete: *Scrabby*
UNDRESSING
  happily watching other people:
  Beaulieu Hill
  unhappily watching other
  people: *Wartnaby*
URGES, violent: *Kent*
URINALS, humiliation at:
  Percyhorner
USELESSNESS
  of acronyms you can never
  remember: *Cafu*
  of bits of the anatomy: *Brecon,*
  Clun
  of business lunches: *Jeffers*
  of dried-up pens: *Kilvaxter*
  of epaulettes: *Trossachs*
  of keys: *Burton Coggles*
  of light switches: *Ockle*
  of raincoats: *Plenmeller*
  of six biros: *Ipplepen*
  of telephones: *Ipswich*
  of three-colour biros: *Ospringe*
  of toasters: *Burnt Yates, Throcking,*
  Throckmorton, Yate
  of trying to attract a barman's
  attention: *Epping*
USHERETTES: *Blean*

V

VAMPIRE ATTACKS: *Spittal of*
  Glenshee
VEGETABLES
  abused by Victorians: *Cong*
  coloured bits of: *Poffley End*
  display of: *Halifax*
VENEER, chipboard: *Mapledurham*
VICARS
  entertainment of: *Bude*
  inclinations of: *Lyminster*

  opinions of: *Dean Funes*
VIRGINS, absence of at weddings:
  Shirmers

W

WADS, misshapen, squashy: *Pudsey*
WAGGLING, theatrical: *Llanelli*
WAITERS
  blind: *Epping*
  blue-blooded: *Zlatibor*
  dozy: *Aynho*
  with better memories than you:
  Kenilworth
WALLETS: *Whasset*
WALLS
  covered in snitters: *Snitterfield*
  held on by little brass latches:
  Tewel
  inexpertly papered: *Lupridge*
  insufficiently thick: *Boinka*
  kitchen, daubed: *Smearisary*
  people who drive you up: *Chaling*
  run into: *Drumsna*
  satisfying: *Skellow*
WALLY, a: *Clovis*
WARTLIKE OBJECTS: *Kirby*
  Misperton
WASHING UP
  failure to finish properly: *Abinger,*
  Radlett
  liquid in tea: *Salween*
  nasty bits in the: *Scullet, Hadzor*
WASPS
  confusion about the colour of:
  Wasp Green
  picnics ruined by: *Swaffham*
  Bulbeck
WAVES
  token: *Sturry*
  unnecessary: *Largoward*
  up trouser: *Malibu*
WAY UP, teeth put back the wrong:
  Gipping
WEDDINGS
  friends of bride at: *Shirmers*
  mess caused by: *Pathstruie*
WEE
  small hours of the night, things
  that go 'ahem' in the: *Taroom*
  small hours of the night, things
  that go bang in the: *Balzan*

small hours of the night, things that gurgle in the: *Bonkle*

WEE-WEE
broad jets of: *Spuzzum*
humorous, artificial: *Barstibley*
inopportune moment to have to have a: *Humby*
strategies for having a: *Lower Peover*

WEEK, day of, deliberate ignorance of: *Abligo*

WELSH RAREBIT, growth on: *Eriboll*

WHITEBAIT, pieces of chewed, flying: *Satterthwaite*

WILLIES, insufficiently waggled: *Piddletrenthide, Botley*

WIND, GONE WITH THE: *Epworth*

WINDCHEATERS: *Savernake*

WING
left: *Quedgeley*
right: *Firebag*

WIPERS, windscreen: *Memphis*

WISDOM, NORMAN: *Frimley*

WOOLF, VIRGINIA: *York*

WORDS
deceptive: *Nossob*
Eskimo: *Anantnag*
hatefulness of certain: *Quoyness*
Indonesian, relaxed: *Toodyay*
people who bang on about: *Ainderby Quernhow*

WORKMAN
cleavage in bottom of: *Ravenna*
fraudulent: *Podebrady*

WOUNDS
doubtful: *Hoddlesdon*

on elbows: *Bures*

WRONG
camera: *Hosmer*
gone terribly: *Ely*
place, heart in the: *Willimantic*
things you're in a mind to get: *Hynish*

Y

YAWNS
badly suppressed: *Wawne*
one who: *Lolland*
things that produce a lot of: *Dolgellau, Rigolet*

YEARNINGS
batty: *Abercrave*
nostalgic: *Aberystwyth*

YES
people who won't quite say: *Yetman, Yesnaby*
people you would like to say: *Low Ardwello*

YES, meaning no: *Yesnaby*

YOUTH
crap about jobs done during: *Pulverbatch*
resentment of unfairly apportioned: *Trunch*

Z

Z, A TO: *Worgret*

Appendix

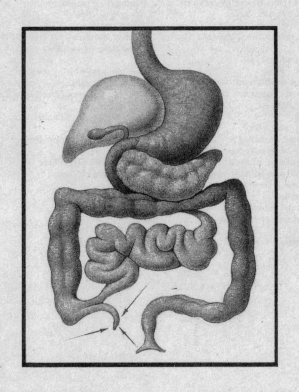